First World War
and Army of Occupation
War Diary
France, Belgium and Germany

5 CAVALRY DIVISION
Divisional Troops
Royal Army Medical Corps
Ambala Cavalry Field Ambulance
1 January 1917 - 31 March 1918

WO95/1163/5

The Naval & Military Press Ltd
www.nmarchive.com
Published in association with The National Archives

Published by

The Naval & Military Press Ltd

Unit 10 Ridgewood Industrial Park,

Uckfield, East Sussex,

TN22 5QE England

Tel: +44 (0) 1825 749494

www.naval-military-press.com

www.nmarchive.com

This diary has been reprinted in facsimile from the original. Any imperfections are inevitably reproduced and the quality may fall short of modern type and cartographic standards.

© **Crown Copyright**
Images reproduced by permission of The National Archives, London, England, 2015.

Contents

Document type	Place/Title	Date From	Date To
Heading	WO95/1163/5		
Heading	5 Cav Div Troops Ambala Cav. Fld Amb 1917 Jan To 1918 Mar		
Heading	War Diary of Ambala Cavalry Field Ambulance 4th Cavalry Division From 1st January 1917 To 31st January 1917		
War Diary	Boubert	01/01/1917	09/01/1917
War Diary	Halloy	11/01/1917	31/01/1917
Heading	From 1-2-1917 to 25th-2-1917 Volumn XXX		
War Diary	Halloy	01/02/1917	28/02/1917
Heading	Ambala C.F.a. 4th Cavalry Division War Diary From 1-3-1917 to 31-3-1917 Volume XXXI		
War Diary	Halloy	01/03/1917	22/03/1917
War Diary	Avenly	23/03/1917	31/03/1917
Heading	Ambala Cavalry Field Ambulance 4th Cav Division From 1-4-1917 to 30-4-1917 Volume XXXII		
War Diary	Aveuly	01/04/1917	03/04/1917
War Diary	Misaumont	05/04/1917	13/04/1917
War Diary	Thievres	14/04/1917	24/04/1917
War Diary	Sarton	25/04/1917	30/04/1917
Heading	War Diary From 1-5-17 to 31-5-17 volume XXXIII Ambala C.F.A 4th Cav Division		
War Diary	Sarton	01/05/1917	14/05/1917
War Diary	Heilly	15/05/1917	15/05/1917
War Diary	Laneuville	16/05/1917	16/05/1917
War Diary	Camped in Quatry near St. Christ	17/05/1917	21/05/1917
War Diary	St. Christ Quarty	21/05/1917	21/05/1917
War Diary	St. Christ	22/05/1917	26/05/1917
War Diary	St. Christ Quarty	26/05/1917	31/05/1917
Heading	War Diary From 1/6/17 to 30/6/17 Volume XXXIV Ambala Cav. Fd, Amb:		
War Diary	Roisel	01/06/1917	29/06/1917
Heading	War Diary From 1/7/17 to 31/7/17 Volume XXXV Ambala Cav Fd. Amb		
War Diary	Roisel	01/07/1917	09/07/1917
War Diary	St. Christ	10/07/1917	31/07/1917
Heading	War Diary From 1/8/17 to 31/8/17 Volume XXXVI Ambala Cav. Fd. Amb		
War Diary	St Christ	01/08/1917	05/08/1917
War Diary	Fourques	07/08/1917	01/09/1917
Heading	War Diary From 1/9/17 to 30/9/17 Volume XXXVII Ambala Cav. Fld. Ambulance		
War Diary	Fourques	01/09/1917	30/09/1917
Heading	War Diary From 1/10/17 to 31/10/17 Vol XXXVIII Ambala Cav. Fld. Amb.		
War Diary	Fourques	01/10/1917	31/10/1917
Heading	War Diary From 1st Nov 1917 to 30 Nov 1917 Vol XXXIX Ambala Cav. Fd. Amb.		
War Diary	Fourques	01/11/1917	20/11/1917
War Diary	Five Concentration Area	21/11/1917	21/11/1917

War Diary	St Ceren	23/11/1917	30/11/1917
War Diary	Villers Faucon	30/11/1917	30/11/1917
Heading	War Diary From 1/12/17 To 31/12/17 Vol XI Ambala Cav. Fd Amb.		
War Diary	St. Cren	01/12/1917	01/12/1917
War Diary	Fourques	04/12/1917	31/12/1917
Heading	War Diary From 1st Jan 1918 To 31 Jan 1918 Vol XLI Ambala Cav Fd. Ambce		
War Diary	Fourques	01/01/1918	09/01/1918
War Diary	Fourques (62 C.V 13a25)	10/01/1918	18/01/1918
War Diary	Fourques	19/01/1918	31/01/1918
Heading	War Diary From 1st Feby 1918 to 28th Feby 1918 vol XLII Ambala cav		
War Diary	Fourques	01/02/1918	01/02/1918
War Diary	Harbonnieres	02/02/1918	02/02/1918
War Diary	Briquemesnil	03/02/1918	03/02/1918
War Diary	Aumont	04/02/1918	28/02/1918
Heading	War Diary From 1-3-1918 to 31-3-1918 Vol. XLIII Ambala C.F.A.		
War Diary	Egypt	01/03/1918	01/03/1918
War Diary	Egypt	16/03/1918	16/03/1918
War Diary	Tel El Kebir	16/03/1918	31/03/1918

WO 95/1163/5

BEF
5 Cav Div Tr[oops]

Ambala
Cav. Fld Amb

~~1916 Jan~~

1917 Jan to 1918 Mar

SERIAL NO. 5

Confidential
War Diary
of

COMMITTEE FOR THE
MEDICAL HISTORY OF THE WAR
Date 23 APR. 1917

AMBALA CAVALRY FIELD AMBULANCE. — 4th Cavalry Division

FROM 1st JANUARY 1917. 1916 TO 31st JANUARY 1917. 1916

WAR DIARY or INTELLIGENCE SUMMARY

Army Form C. 2118.

Place	Date	Hour	Summary of Events and Information	Remarks and references to Appendices
Roulers	1.1.19		Owing to the absence of the wheelers at Divisional H.2. having great difficulty in building latrines now organised Wrote for card passes to A.P.M. for Motor cyclists. Refers (3) Gunning No 33532 Pr Sullivan of S.C., H.S. reported his arrival today and was taken on the strength.	
	2.1.19		Replied to A.D.M.S. that no Shotguns have been indented for by this unit since the reorganisation of the corps. The British ovation form and the canteen are proving great successes and are enough appreciated by the men Again wrote about the difficulty caused by the removal of the wheeler & painter out to two have been only returned when we were moving would only be a hindrance without an assistance as all would not be able to carry on his duties then and his lorry lot tool box and kennels would have to be carried on the ambulance waggons	
	5.1.19		asked RSO Sublet Rde. if any lorry was to make up deficiency of coal	

T./134. Wt. W708-776. 500000. 4/15. Sir J.C. & S.

Army Form C. 2118.

WAR DIARY
or
INTELLIGENCE SUMMARY.
(Erase heading not required.)

Instructions regarding War Diaries and Intelligence Summaries are contained in F. S. Regs., Part II. and the Staff Manual respectively. Title pages will be prepared in manuscript.

Place	Date	Hour	Summary of Events and Information	Remarks and references to Appendices
Boulout	5.1.17		Wrote again about R/116 & sent to Deputy Commissioner Ambala District to settle left of place about which Rahman on 20 Dec 17.15 and next no knowledge. Again asked for the Horse Ambulance which is supposed to be undergoing alterations to make it carry 4 wheels instead laying intend 2 only. Also for the G.S.Wagon undergoing alterations.	
			Driver David returned from leave.	
	7.1.17		Sent correction of figures of men & animals to 34 D.M.S. copy of letter showing numbers in ambulance in case of entrainment. Wrote very urgent to Staff Capt. Whose Bde asking when & where he wanted horses from that ambulance for the Pioneer Bn. Received no reply.	
	9.1.17		Proceeded to Kacaratin from Boulout leading the ambulance office about a quarter to eleven in the morning after seeing the	

WAR DIARY
or
INTELLIGENCE SUMMARY.
(Erase heading not required.)

Place	Date	Hour	Summary of Events and Information	Remarks and references to Appendices
Boulogne	9.1.17		correspondence and orders that had come up in order to give evidence at a Court Martial that was being held at the 6th Innuskilling Dragoons headquarters. Capt. Lang R.A.M.C. left on duty, he was busy getting at claims which I had previously asked of for damages. The packing of the G.S. Wagons was proceeding but several boxes had to be left until the springs (the indent for which had only just arrived at D.M.S.) had been received from the medical store depot. I had to return by 1 P.M. as I had been warned that my evidence (would be called early) on arrival at Boulogne through doubts that I would be called till 2 P.M. at 10 minutes to 2 P.M. recieving letters from [illegible] cyclist anying orders say to be received to entrain as soon as ready, this letter had been much delayed owing to one cyclist being with A.D.M.S.	

WAR DIARY
or
INTELLIGENCE SUMMARY.
(Erase heading not required.)

Army Form C. 2118.

Place	Date	Hour	Summary of Events and Information	Remarks and references to Appendices
Bombay	9.1.17		Letter that out on duty. You in my absence at least wanted Capt. Long had again main tonic time enquiries to entrain handed to telephone R.T.O. Yframand Engineer, which I did & received reply expected at 3 P.M. (It was then 2.15 P.M.) I replied that owing to it snowing & pestows being at least 8 miles out to expect us before 6 P.M. Received a reply that would not do but the ambulance should be entrained before dark as it would be better to start entraining at 5 A.M. next morning. Asked why we had not been informed before & received a reply this arrangement had been made with Divisional Sny 10.30 A.M. that morning at latest. Telephoned A.D.M.S. & asked me was it correct that we should entrain that evening & was it would be impossible to do so before dark & also R.T.O. had said that would not do. Received reply to get down to Mombout as soon as possible. Proceed at once to Bombart	

Place	Date	Hour	Summary of Events and Information	Remarks and references to Appendices
Baghdad	9.1.17		where I found everything packed & great moving of 2.45 P.m. An ambulance moved out received third order from A.D.M.S. not to move & entrain till 5 A.M. next morning. Capt Kay showed me to what orders he had received during my absence. 1st one from S.A. D.M.S. ordering entrainment next morning at 5 A.M. next morning. 2nd [Cancel] the 2 A.M. 24 the British had gone to take their food and the Indians to cook food for that meal for the next day as well as although rations had been sent for three days no mention was made of woodcoal which we usually had to cool her own. 2nd one to Sialkot Bde Headquarters to divert & which of course could not now be done. At 12.10 P.M. another message arrived saying your train is in march to Khushrut and entrain today. Orders were immediately issued but	

Army Form C. 2118.

WAR DIARY
or
INTELLIGENCE SUMMARY.
(Erase heading not required.)

Place	Date	Hour	Summary of Events and Information	Remarks and references to Appendices
Bardwell	9.1.17		owing to all the medical officers being out on duty except Capt Long and the men away having their food & the Indians left their billet at the end of village cooking pot the most long & most important of all the difficulty of finding an interpreter to give orders to Indians, the O.C. & the Indian Officers (tho' being away on duty) some delay was unavoidably experienced so that the ambulance was not actually on the move till 2.45 P.M. It was snowing hard all the time the waggons were being packed and the driving party was 10 made the kahars alone. No assistance could be given by the motor drivers as all seven cars and two motor cyclists were out on duty, as well as the medical officers. On receipt of the third order to wait till next morning the waggons were taken to the top of the hill & parked there. Orders were issued to march at 1.30 A.M. on the 10th —	

WAR DIARY
or
INTELLIGENCE SUMMARY

Army Form C. 2118.

Place	Date	Hour	Summary of Events and Information	Remarks and references to Appendices
Hallay	10.1.17		The Ambulance duly marched from Beaulest at 1.30 A.M. Two officers and 11 I.O.R's also being left behind to go in the motors direct. The K.O.S.M. went in times about 4 P.M. saying that when he came to take over the train from the R.T.O. (re the R.T.O. told him the train had been broken up & would not be ready till next morning. Sent off 2nd K.O.S.M. Mirza again to either take over the train or receive a written reply from the R.T.O. that there was no train to take over, also to sent dismounted men & extra days rations. On starting on march to Mouraut it seemed most trying on animals & feet were unusually softening (tally balls). Three horses were taken on the march & by the time the wagons drove into the station yard it was 4.45 A.M. No resistance was given by the railway staff except that two flares were manoeuvred by them. A movable	

WAR DIARY or INTELLIGENCE SUMMARY

Army Form C. 2118.

Place	Date	Hour	Summary of Events and Information	Remarks and references to Appendices
Halloy	11.1.17		ramp was used for animals but owing to snow & mud it was both slippery & difficult to move & in the dark the animals were slipping about with balls of melting snow under their feet so the sixteen wagons & fray ramp which could accommodate two trucks, one sideways and one end ways, on a turn table, were provided but the ramp was deep in mud & snow & it was difficult to man-handle the loaded wagons up it & the trucks had great trouble across their floors over which the 16 wagons had to be pulled. The R.T.O. was unable to say if not wagons would be in the on each truck so the trucks were in single width wasted nearly half an hour of our time by wanting that he had previously fitted four of our shaft limbers on a truck & insisted on it being done until it	

Army Form C. 2118.

WAR DIARY
or
INTELLIGENCE SUMMARY.
(Erase heading not required.)

Place	Date	Hour	Summary of Events and Information	Remarks and references to Appendices
Hollay	11.1.17		proved impossible. He had meant artillery limbers & did not realise ours were larger. The want of experienced officers & sergeants was much felt as well with insuperable difficulty of the language, sto officer except the C.O. having interpreter at all entraining & both transport sergeants not being able to speak to Indians or ever had charge during an entraining & all the trained officers & sergeants having been change recently. At 6 A.M. the R.T.O. for the first time informed me that he had orders to us to be entrained by 7 A.M. no previous intimation having ever been given that 7 a.m. was the hour at which the ambulance would be expected to be entrained. Two hours in a snow storm in the dark with a unit from which every of the British officers & sergeants & warrant officers to who could speak Hindustani had	

WAR DIARY or INTELLIGENCE SUMMARY

Army Form C. 2118.

Place	Date	Hour	Summary of Events and Information	Remarks and references to Appendices
Halles	11.1.17		been sent recently to induce so that practically half the unit cannot speak to the other half. Was not in my opinion time enough to enable it to complete the whole ambulance was entrained by 8 A.M. but the train was not dispatched by the R.T.O. till 2 A.M. The train arrived at Malincourt about 9.30 P.M. & the ambulance detrained at once in the dark in 2 hours, no lights or flares were allowed. The ambulance then marched to here the long journey at 2 A.M. in the morning in a bitter cold night. It was informed that no accommodation for men or animals could be given but for the men they might use the canvas covers huts but must be ready to turn out at any time as a battalion was expected in the huts & sixteen Bell tents would be issued to us. The animals will not today take their food properly so I have got them behind a wall for protection	

WAR DIARY
or
INTELLIGENCE SUMMARY.

Army Form C. 2118.

Place	Date	Hour	Summary of Events and Information	Remarks and references to Appendices
Holley Hpt	14.1.17		Still snowing and bitterly cold. Capt Lang & 2/Lt Sahai marched with "A" Section of the ambulance to Hauptreille 17 miles away to look after the Ambala Pioneer Battalion belonging to the Vth Ind Div. at present attached VIIth Corps, while we are looking after the Mhow & Sialkot Pioneer Btns. belonging to the IVth Ind Div attached VIIth Corps. We are having trouble about the Rat voles to-day by the VIIth Corps as they forgot to close the loop doors of windows and the vermin got/did not meet with a jolt. The engineers having built up we shall have to dismantle it and put it up. Surmise is again on the floor which we have now obtained. / L	
	15.1.17		Pte Wilson G.b. D.J. Promoted on leave to England. Completed hospital hut today. C.O. went on some Visits 20 degrees of frost at night. Half the animals have been	

WAR DIARY or INTELLIGENCE SUMMARY

Army Form C. 2118.

(Erase heading not required.)

Place	Date	Hour	Summary of Events and Information	Remarks and references to Appendices
Wallon	15/1/17		Got under cover including all the horses, got all the remainder on 2 from G. Lansburg under the lee of a hedge.	
	16/1/17		Two Indian patients admitted & sent on to the dressing C.C.S. by car. Have had to alter hut.	
	19/1/17		D.Roach returned from leave to England today and tent again comp[lete]d. Two new huts constructed to replace old ones.	
	20/1/17		Three motor ambulance cars left with a - two Dis. returned & two sent to Capt. Long with 3rd A.R.C.	
	21/1/17		Two Indian patients admitted, but tent is rebuilt fairly comfortable & no any but 2 old Canadian stoves were very wasteful of fuel & not lasting well.	
	22/1/17		Seven Indian patients admitted nearly all bronchitis from the desperately cold beastly wind. No 6 Germany went to C.A. station on the Bryce journey.	

WAR DIARY or INTELLIGENCE SUMMARY

Army Form C. 2118.

Place	Date	Hour	Summary of Events and Information	Remarks and references to Appendices
Hollay	24.1.17		Two Indian patients admitted (1) all British are being packed up by us & sent by rest to O/C 98 Field Ambulance. Sgt Major Cooke R.A.M.C. sent to join C.H. Section. 25 Krishna Menur to proceed on leave to England. One Indian patient admitted (Tac)	
	25.1.17			
	26.1.17		Three Indian patients admitted.	
	27.1.17		Three Indian patients admitted (1). Two cases of gonorrhoea & two of bronchitis sent to Lucknow C.S. & I went myself to see at D.M.S. & met the 14, 14, 2, 3, 4, 7, 4, 4.2	
	28.1.17		Returned from to Division me for ambulance truck was spring on return journey & I had to borrow a motor ambulance from 33rd Field ambulance to return & were to C.B. Supply & to send for bithen to 15 Sahawn left to join Base school at Noiget hady matter 15 Hudson sent to take 15 Sahawn place with 4 motors an	
	29.1.17		left alone with 1/3 K.C. orators of ambulance	

Army Form C. 2118.

WAR DIARY
or
INTELLIGENCE SUMMARY.
(Erase heading not required.)

Instructions regarding War Diaries and Intelligence Summaries are contained in F. S. Regs., Part II. and the Staff Manual respectively. Title pages will be prepared in manuscript.

Place	Date	Hour	Summary of Events and Information	Remarks and references to Appendices
Hallay	29.1.17		Two patients admitted, four evacuated to Lucknow C.C.S	
	30.1.17		One patient admitted & four evacuated to Lucknow C.C.S. Have been given a thirteen Bow hut in addition to hospital, much warmer though smaller hut than VII's Corps hut. Treated whole hut in one day. Moved all remaining patients into it.	
	31.1.17		12.33.530 Pte Welsh 1st Bn 4 S.C. H.I. evacuated for otitis media. Three patients admitted.	

E.C. Hodgson Maj. I.M.S.
Comdg. Ambala Cavalry Field Ambulance

ORIGINAL

MEDICAL

Serial No: 5

From 1-2-1914 to 28-2-1914

COMMITTEE FOR THE MEDICAL HISTORY OF THE WAR
Date 21 MAY 1917

VOLUMN XXX

War Diary of Ambala C.F.A. 4th Cavalry Division

E.C. Hodgson Maj.
I.M.S.
O.C. Ambala Csv. Fd. Amb.

Army Form C. 2118.

WAR DIARY
or
INTELLIGENCE SUMMARY.

(Erase heading not required.)

Instructions regarding War Diaries and Intelligence Summaries are contained in F. S. Regs., Part II. and the Staff Manual respectively. Title pages will be prepared in manuscript.

Place	Date	Hour	Summary of Events and Information	Remarks and references to Appendices
Halloy	1st Feb.		Weather extremely cold 25-30 degrees of frost at night, freezing all day, and a bitter East wind continually blowing. This is the coldest weather we have experienced since the begining of the war at least in France, and the whole ambulance in the poorest billets they have ever had, the animals having been put in the open just after they had been clipped, in accordance with orders, and the personel in low and single fly canvas huts, muddy floors, which are now sheeted with ice inside from the moisture in the mens breath as the cold has lasted now more than three weeks. The men of the Pioneer battalions are relieved by the Division and return to good billets but the Ambulance being the only complete unit up is not relieved. A certan number of true cases of frostbite have occured among Indians with loss of skin and subcutaneous tissues of the ball of the fingers or great toe but no permanent injuries so far. No cases have occured amongst the Ambulance personel. I am experiencing some difficulty in obtaining supplies from the D.A.D.O.S. 30-th vi Di\sion of ordinance stores. Under present arrangements when it is necessary	A.C.W

Army Form C. 2118.

WAR DIARY
or
INTELLIGENCE SUMMARY.
(Erase heading not required.)

Instructions regarding War Diaries and Intelligence Summaries are contained in F.S. Regs., Part II. and the Staff Manual respectively. Title pages will be prepared in manuscript.

Place	Date	Hour	Summary of Events and Information	Remarks and references to Appendices
Hallay	1.2.17		to evacuate Indian sick from the Ambulance they are sent down in motor ambulance cars belonging No 3 M.A.C. to the Lucknow C.C.S. at Fressenneville 40 miles away. British sick are sent to No 97 Field Ambulance Mondicourt. The animals are still on only $\frac{3}{4}$ ration of oats (9lbs.) and the hay is often short too and they are showing it, I reported it to the A.A. & Q.M.G. when he was up here from the 4th Division and he promised to do what was possible but the horse ration has not improved. Indian sick in ambulance 8, evacuated nil. Sent sputum of 4 cases of bronchitis for examination for tubercle. Sent one case for X ray.	
	2.2.17		Complained to A.D.V.S. 30th DIV. of shortage of rations for animals and want of stabling and asked again if he could assist us in any way but he replied he could not nor give me permission to buy straw to make up when the hay was short. Ø Indian patients in the hospital 1 admitted, 10 remaining.	

Army Form C. 2118.

WAR DIARY
or
INTELLIGENCE SUMMARY.

(Erase heading not required.)

Place	Date	Hour	Summary of Events and Information	Remarks and references to Appendices
Hellry	3.2.17		Telegram recieved from A.D.M.S. 4th Cav. Div. saying Ambulance struck off divisional leave roster placed on 3rd Army roster, wrote at once to D.M.S. though A.D.M.S. 50th Div. enclosing nominal roll. Indian patients in hospital admitted 1, remained 11.	
	4.2.17		Gradually getting all the animals under shelter as troops in village change. Indian patients in hospital, 3 admitted, 4 evacuated, 10 remained.	
	5.2.17		38th C.I.H. had an outbreak of diarrhoea in its Sikh squadrons last night due I think to dirty cooking pots, treated with castor oil all seem better. Orders recieved to send sergeant Mitchell & daf. Imam Ali for a refresher course to Gas School. Lt Sahai I.M.S.(T.C.) having been invalided to England the affects of cold, is struck off the Ambulance, Lt Krishnamoorty who was on leave in Enland has written to say he has been admitted to No 3 London general hospital from the effects of the same, these officers are not fit to stand the climate out here they are quite a different race and class from the men.	

Army Form C. 2118.

WAR DIARY
or
INTELLIGENCE SUMMARY.
(Erase heading not required.)

Instructions regarding War Diaries and Intelligence Summaries are contained in F. S. Regs., Part II. and the Staff Manual respectively. Title pages will be prepared in manuscript.

Place	Date	Hour	Summary of Events and Information	Remarks and references to Appendices
Mallery	5.2.17		Indian patients in hospital To Duty 3, Remained 7.	
	6.2.17		Driver Bunt and driver Eyre were brought to the Orderly Room and informed that driver Bunt had had his sentence by court martial remitted Eyre suspended for another 3 months. Referred O.C.,"D.D.Remounts to 4th Cav. Div. because he was unable in W.E. to find our present composition. Again wrote to D.A.D.O.S. 30th Div. about hastening supply of ordinance stores. Again wrote about leave for British in which is being given to Pioneer Bat. but not to us. Indians patients in hospital 1 admitted , 8 remaining .	
	7.2.17		Sent Field Cashier 4th Cav. Div. the sum of F.2071 - 10C.for 26 macintoshes for British and 76 for Indians. Recieved last night at 10.30 P.M. from A.D.M.S. 4th C.D. letters dated 2nd, 3rd, 4th, 5th, 6th, and a wire asking why I had not anwered the earlier ones , I am making enqiries at the signal office. Indian patients in hospital 2 admitted , 10 remained .	

WAR DIARY
or
INTELLIGENCE SUMMARY.
(Erase heading not required.)

Army Form C. 2118.

Place	Date	Hour	Summary of Events and Information	Remarks and references to Appendices
Kalloy	8.2.17		Reported to A.D.M.S. 4th C.D. that I had no accommodation for infectious cases except tents which I considered unsafe for Indians owing to the bitter cold which still continues. Asked for another medical officer to replace one of my casualties as we have been reduced to three officers for the last three weeks and with one section away I have been trying to carry on by myself. O.C. Signals 7th Corps reports A.D.M.S. letters recieved for despatch on evening of 4/4 6th am forwarding the letter. Indians sick in hospital, 3 admitted, 5 eacuated, 8 remained.	
	9.2.17		Wired to D.AD.O.S. 30th Div. for ordinance stores indented for but not recieved, no reply. Asked bacteriologist No 8 Mobile Laboratory to take blood cultures from three cases of suspected Enteric fever. Indians sick in Hospital 4 admitted, 1 to duty, 11 remained.	
	10.2.17		Driver Welsh attd. from Aux. Horse Transport, evacuated sick with Otitis Media and struck off our strength. No 2 Cook Himtia dhp Jodpur Lancers died in the hospital from general bronchitis and was burnt. Indians sick in hospital 1 admitted, 4 evacuated, 8 remained.	

Army Form C. 2118.

WAR DIARY
or
INTELLIGENCE SUMMARY.
(Erase heading not required.)

Instructions regarding War Diaries and Intelligence Summaries are contained in F. S. Regs., Part II. and the Staff Manual respectively. Title pages will be prepared in manuscript.

Place	Date	Hour	Summary of Events and Information	Remarks and references to Appendices
Halloy	11.2.17		Indians in hospital , 3 admitted , 1 died , 10 remained .	
			No 8 Mobile Laboratory all bloods from suspected Enterics negative .	
			No leave allotment yet given to this Ambulance , I have written twice.	
			Motor ambulances constantly breaking down due to bolts and top leaves of springs giving way on the frozen roads .	
	12.2.17		Received a wire saying ordinance store now to be obtained 6th Corps . Supplies and every thing much to obtain at A section under 6th Corps easier than here . Indians sick in hospital , to duty 1, evacuated 4, 5 remained.	
	13.2.17		Again wrote and went and saw D.D.M.S. 7th Corps about leave , all say we do not come on their list but cannot inform me where to apply for it . Went and saw R.E. in charge of pioneer work who said he would have put us on his list if he had been informed of our being here like he was of the other units. He would put our name down but leave was now closed .	
			Indians in hospital , 1 admitted , 5 remained .	

A5834 Wt.W4973/M687 750,000 8/16 D.D.& L. Ltd. Forms/C.2118/13

Army Form C. 2118.

WAR DIARY
or
INTELLIGENCE SUMMARY.

(Erase heading not required.)

Instructions regarding War Diaries and Intelligence Summaries are contained in F. S. Regs., Part II. and the Staff Manual respectively. Title pages will be prepared in manuscript.

Place	Date	Hour	Summary of Events and Information	Remarks and references to Appendices
Mailly	14.2.17		Indians in hospital , 2 admitted , 8 remained .	JCH
	15.2.17		D.A.D.O.S. 30th Div. now writes to inform me that 5th Corps are supplying A section of this Ambulance at Haupteville and not us , the ordinance supply is getting more and more behind I have written strongly about it . Indians in hospital , 3 admitted , 11 remained .	JCH
	16.2.17		Indians in hospital , 3 admitted , 2 to duty , 4 evacuated , 8 remained.	JCH
	17.2.17		The Secunderabad Pioneer Battalion has arrived so the ambulance is now looking after 3 battalions here and one at Hautenville . I have recalled L- Hudson . Have had canvas beds made for the hospital they are more comfortable and take up less space than stretchers . Indians in hospital , 4 evacuated , 4 remained .	JCH
	18.2.17		Indians in hospital , 1 admitted , 5 remained .	JCH
	19.2.17		Indians in hospital , 5 remained .	JCH

Army Form C. 2118.

WAR DIARY
or
INTELLIGENCE SUMMARY.
(Erase heading not required.)

Instructions regarding War Diaries and Intelligence Summaries are contained in F. S. Regs., Part II. and the Staff Manual respectively. Title pages will be prepared in manuscript.

Place	Date	Hour	Summary of Events and Information	Remarks and references to Appendices
Mallory	20.2/17		The thaw has at last come and in spite of the thaw scheme the roads are in a terrible condition and the huts are dripping water on the unfortunate men, sweeper Nanak has died of bronchitis in Lucknow C.C.S. he had 35 years government service and was a good worker and is a loss to the ambulance. Indians in hospital, 2 admitted, 0 7 remained.	
	21.2.17		Again wrote to D.A.D.O.S. 30th Div. a strong letter. Indians in hospital, 2 admitted, 9 remained,	
	22.2.17		Recieved new combined circular on anti-gas measures. Indians in hospital, 3 admitted, 2 to duty, evacuated 4, 6 remained	
	23.2.17		A Echelon to be changed leaving out all cooks carts and only taking 3 limbers. Indians in hospital, 6 remained.	
	24.2.17		Wrote a long letter to the D.A.D.O.S. 30th Div. giving copies of all my indents and pointings out how impossible it was to carry on as at present supplied. pro-pose asking permission to take the matter up to "Q"branch if my letter has no effect.	

Army Form C. 2118.

WAR DIARY
or
INTELLIGENCE SUMMARY.

(Erase heading not required.)

Instructions regarding War Diaries and Intelligence Summaries are contained in F. S. Regs., Part II. and the Staff Manual respectively. Title pages will be prepared in manuscript.

Place	Date	Hour	Summary of Events and Information	Remarks and references to Appendices
Halloy	24.2.17		Indians in hospital , 1 admitted , 1 to duty , 8 remained .	AA/H
	25.2.17		All grooms and batmen belonging to officers in ambulances are under orders to be replaced by inferior men, have written to A.D.M.S. 4-th C.D. pointing out how serious this will be as they all belong to the mounted pack section and are accustomed to working with our Indians and some of them speak a few words of Hindustani . 8 Indians in hospital , 2 admitted , 2 evacuated , 6 remained .	AA/H
	26.2.17		Indians in hospital , 2 admitted , 8 remained ,	AA/H
	27.2.17		Changing Pte. Prosser for motorcyclist instead of Pte. Gunning who in my opinion is too heavy on these bad roads . Indians in hospital , 1 evacuated , 7 remained .	AA/H
	28.2.17		Indians in hospital , 4 admitted , 2 to duty , 9 remained .	AA/H

Serial No. 5

MEDICAL

ORIGINAL
Mar. 1917

War Diary from 1-3-1917 to 31-3-1917

VOLUME XXXI

Ambala C. F. Q. 4th Cavalry Division

COMMITTEE FOR THE
MEDICAL HISTORY OF THE WAR
Date — 6 JUL. 1917

T. C. Hodgson Maj.
I.M.S.
O.C. Ambala C.F.A.

WAR DIARY
or
INTELLIGENCE SUMMARY.
(Erase heading not required.)

Army Form C. 2118.

Place	Date	Hour	Summary of Events and Information	Remarks and references to Appendices
Halloy	1.3.17		Lt MacKay R.A.M.C. reported his arrival and was taken on the strength.	
	2.3.17		Lt MacKay went to join A Section at Huntsville under Capt Long R.A.M.C.	
	4.3.17		Evacuated 4 Indian Sick to Lucknow C.C.S. Trescanville. There is very little sickness now in the Pioneer Bdes. The D. A.D.O.S. 30 Div. his again a/tized my indent & sent us the wrong type for the horse ambulance as that we just went without of the proper type & it will take some time to get new ones. Changed motor cyclist from P.C. Gunning to Pte Rogers as Gunnings triangle cross-arm breaking owing to his weight. Put up suggestion to A. D.M.S. 4 & C Div that my particulars stores on the following changes:— (1) That as none but limbered wagons may be issued to A Echelon and both cook carts of the ambulance are of G.S. Wagons that on limbered field kitchen be supplied in	

WAR DIARY
or
INTELLIGENCE SUMMARY.
(Erase heading not required.)

Army Form C. 2118.

Place	Date	Hour	Summary of Events and Information	Remarks and references to Appendices
Prulloy	4.3.17		Place of one G.S. wagon urgently as carrying fittgs are only to form advanced dressing stations at present. (2) That two water carts be taken instead of one. (3) That four animals be issued for each horse ambulance because two cannot possibly draw them on heavy ground. That is experience on the Somme last year, having proved that (4) That is the leading limb of animals with the indents sent in. 13 echelon wagon (last year) when left behind on A echelon moving forward, was taken for this purpose — medical units should there be taken forward to supply the needed extra animals, one for the 3 limbers, viz. four for the horse ambulances.	
	6.3.17		Sent Pte Crazy J 19th D.G. with two horses to join 14th Port. Lgt Dy by rail. Very little is known in Division re the work seems to men (them more that the autumn jobs have started.) There is most shortage of saddlers, particularly for Indians.	

Army Form C. 2118.

WAR DIARY
or
INTELLIGENCE SUMMARY.
(Erase heading not required.)

Place	Date	Hour	Summary of Events and Information	Remarks and references to Appendices
Halloy	11.3.17		Sent down motor cyclist Fraser with Triumph motor cycle to 4 Cav. Div. Workshop to have it changed for a Douglas in accordance with orders.	
	14.3.17		Four Indian sick evacuated. Wrote for permit for Fraser's cycle in place of old Triumph as no Douglas would ever be at Workshop.	
	15.3.17		D.r Billany (Tues) by C.M. for not being present at 7 A.M parade and 2 rity with making a false statement to Pte J.S. re kit returns to Depot.	
			D.r Billing sentenced to 7 days F.P.1 Field Punishment on &c charge. Have scheme again working owing to the complete state of the roads which means all rations have to known on limbs. Waymouth on mulehead & no lorries & motor ambulances to be using. Heard that all our horses but Indian, who we have not see anything of # several orders to return today to the Sqn A+ Cav. Div., as there were no orders for us, wrote & asked for them from 3 S.D Div. & 7 Corps, whomever	

WAR DIARY
INTELLIGENCE SUMMARY
(Erase heading not required.)

Army Form C. 2118.

Place	Date	Hour	Summary of Events and Information	Remarks and references to Appendices
Hallory	17.3.17		Evacuated (2) ill sick to Turkson C.C.S yesterday. Asked D.D.M.S. VI Corps to return A. Salon from Trevilla which has just arrived. Reply received from D.D.M.S VI – Corps that my orders had been received for the unit. Wired the A.D.M.S 4th Cav: Div asking if any mobile for me.	
	20.3.17		Increasing difficulty about getting supplies of all kinds, horses particularly badly fed & showing the effect, plus of firewood & fresh food for Indians. Can get no information where our Division have moved. Wired & wrote D.D.M.S. 7th Division, Lefford/th also WhoC VII– Corps & H.Q. to D by am asking for orders. 9.30. Div on 17th about supply lines increasing difficulty – 4 / n–C to D. L.D.J.S 3rd Cav Div old soulmates (& Cotts). Indian ration wady lost on British. To bring to him hump & was leaving it until team May 17. Reply.	
	22.3.17	6 P.M	First drawn orders to march tomorrow & join A.D. Cav Bde at villages. March to have necessary orders on road to him 4/5 (from Ammunition).	
Armay	23.3.17			

Army Form C. 2118.

WAR DIARY
or
INTELLIGENCE SUMMARY.
(Erase heading not required.)

Place	Date	Hour	Summary of Events and Information	Remarks and references to Appendices
Arundy	23.3.17		and join the Sialkot Bde at Arundy. Roads broken but the march, 23 miles, accomplished without difficulty. Reinforcement	
	26.4.17		All P.H. & helmets changed for small box type. Each man fitted & tested with gas hat. We are living in huts with horses under some shelter, weather extremely bad. Have now joined our own Brigade, the Mhow Fd. In accordance with S.A.D.M.S. & OC D's orders sent out eight carts for use with O Battery. I.K. Mortly reported suspicious from aeroplane. Have been washing head of m Manion(?) Both section which is to go forward with brigade. It is composed of following left. Capt. Legg & Lt. Mackay. Having orderly Baxter, 3 hdly. Mil. Serje Perin, 18 men mounted, leading two Indian ponies on the packs containing eight gallons of water, dressings, drugs medical comforts, cylinders & 4 hand stretchers. All men trained, a first aid, carrying in foot harness, &m carrying all splints for Advanced dressing station in long canvas bags	
	30.4.17		behind sent off [?] horse ambulance. L.F. Bennee & 4 M.E. (F.A.) reported to arrival from 4 = Art Bde #2 K (was to been in the strength of)	

Army Form C. 2118.

WAR DIARY
or
INTELLIGENCE SUMMARY.
(Erase heading not required.)

Instructions regarding War Diaries and Intelligence Summaries are contained in F. S. Regs., Part II. and the Staff Manual respectively. Title pages will be prepared in manuscript.

Place	Date	Hour	Summary of Events and Information	Remarks and references to Appendices
Aveluy	31.3.17		All such British & Indians are being evacuated to 1/2 Australian 3/ Ambulance Becordel. Reserves orders to move to Mcraucourt today since cancelled. Asked for copies of all approved maps for this area & beyond where fighting likely to take place from Staff Capt. Minor 43 div	

T. C. Hodgson Major D.M.S
O.C. Ambulance C. F. A.

ORIGINAL
April 1917

MEDICAL
Serial No. 5.

War Diary from 1-4-1917 to 30-4-1917

VOLUME XXXII

Ambala Cavalry Field Ambulance 4th Cav Division.

COMMITTEE FOR THE
MEDICAL HISTORY OF THE WAR.
Date -6 JUL 1917

T.C. Hodgson

Army Form C. 2118

WAR DIARY
or
INTELLIGENCE SUMMARY.
(Erase heading not required.)

Place	Date	Hour	Summary of Events and Information	Remarks and references to Appendices
Acheux	1.4.17		Not having been with the unit when dumps of kit etc were made, the unit made a dump at Senlis where costs but was left under charge of Town Major. SOH	
	3.4.17		The following joined the unit — A.V.C. 1775 D.B. Forage " 2209 Bhoremmah M.T. 7/2014 Sweeper Behara Six horses were taken away by orders of A.D.V.S. 4th C.D. to be handed to 36th Field Horse. Left the D.S. only took four. Marched to camp near Miraumont with where R. Pole sent fin of motor Amb. cars (to be temporarily attached between C.F.A. as wards to base). Sweeper Jayah when going from Sans-sout over 50 yds old, quite unable to march reported it to A.D.M.S.	SOH SOH
Miraumont	5.4.17		Sergt Harona A.S.C, M.T. sent sick to N.Z 9 C.C.S. has been evacuated to base & is struck off the ambulance	SOH

WAR DIARY
or
INTELLIGENCE SUMMARY

Army Form C. 2118.

Place	Date	Hour	Summary of Events and Information	Remarks and references to Appendices
Monument	5.4.17		Found a mule staying in our lines very lame from cracked heels, reported it. We are all under canvas here, weather very cold & changeable with snow-storms. Moved all instances ('to Minnimus')	
	7.4.17		Weather still very changeable, no sick during admitted into our own & hospital but sent direct to C.C.S. Moving to-night to Sapignie with A. Echelon, M. Faction to join Mhoin C. Bde.	
	9.4.17			
	11.4.17		The march to Sapignie and back was carried out under considerable difficulties as roads very bad & repeated snow-storms. Cavalry not used in advance. Marched to Mory water & took mules over worse conditions starting at 6 A.M & returning at midnight, heavy mod: storms to-night roads blocked with traffic, animals showing exhaustion. Subject long roll in action for a short time, 19 casualties	
Ytrnes	14.4.17		Marched here yesterday, good billets & places for horses. A little difficulty owing to no responsible officer kindly firsts 15 Echelon.	

WAR DIARY or INTELLIGENCE SUMMARY

Army Form C. 2118.

Place	Date	Hour	Summary of Events and Information	Remarks and references to Appendices
Thièvres	17/4/17		Major E.C. Hodgson J.M.S. left for 10 days leave. Letter from D.H.Q. Northern stated of embarkation from 18th inst. until 25th arrived after Major Hodgson's departure. Hospital was moved to better quarters.	
Thièvres	18/4/17		Two motor ambulances sudden reported to workshops at Albert for repair. A.D.M.S. 17th division inspected the unit, particularly Harnesses and hospital. The harness are now visibly improved in condition since removal into the present billets. Pte. Bryce O.S.S.C. M.T. admitted to hospital c/o with P.U.O. &	Bt/Staff RAMC Staff RAMC
Thièvres	19/4/17			Staff RAMC
Thièvres	20/4/17		nothing	
"	21/4/17		Motor Amb workshops. The motor ambulances returned from workshops at Albert, repaired. There was the ambulance referred to on 18th inst. The A.D.M.S. in Gen. Orders notified the hospital of this foremoon. A horse-ambulance is to be kept to collect sick from Authie (6 Pym) and Marieux. (D.M.O.)	Staff RAMC

WAR DIARY
or
INTELLIGENCE SUMMARY.
(Erase heading not required.)

Army Form C. 2118

Instructions regarding War Diaries and Intelligence Summaries are contained in F. S. Regs., Part II. and the Staff Manual respectively. Title pages will be prepared in manuscript.

Place	Date	Hour	Summary of Events and Information	Remarks and references to Appendices
Thievres	2.4.17		Two motor ambulances proceeded to A.D.M.S. for duties. Pte Bothell, R.S.C., M.T. was evacuated sick with pyrexia (influenza?) — Pte Brown A.S.C. M.T. was discharged from hospital & rejoined for duty.	
Thievres	3.4.17		This Unit was inspected and found in good condition by Colonel Gore-Langton (A.D.M.S. 46th Div.) He did not however find fault with the welfare of horses and mules.	
Thievres	24.4.17		Hospital gear inspected this morning by O. I/c Tns., 2nd Army. Orders were received in the evening to move to huts in Acton 0-mile road. The unit marched there this forenoon leaving Thievres at 10.30 am and ordinary hours without incident at 11.15 am. At 12.30 pm. orders were received while in billets to move from billets at Thievres and take over huts. Ample accommodation exists at present. Three huts are used as hospital — 2 for British, 1 for Indian sick. Horses are in covered standings with city of	
Sinton	25.4.17			

Army Form C. 2118.

WAR DIARY
or
INTELLIGENCE SUMMARY.
(Erase heading not required.)

Place	Date	Hour	Summary of Events and Information	Remarks and references to Appendices
Sialkot	26/4/17		Stone floors. Dr Bruce returned from leave this morning. Lt. A. Burns inspected the hospital and billets just after and arrived in our new billets.	RML
Sialkot	27/4/17		Nothing of note happened to-day.	RML
Sialkot	28/4/17		Nothing of note happened to-day. Weather continues excellent. Horses Ashwin have now been grazing daily for some time and for the most part very fit.	RML
Sialkot	29/4/17		Major Horsfryn arrived back from leave this afternoon. On W.d. Orderly No. 1378, Sowar Joo-Singh Jaithia and one Sweeper [illegible] have been evacuated as unfrements & replace those evacuated.	RML
Sialkot	30/4/17		Took over from Capt Long R.A.M.C. (I.C.) on return from 10 days leave. Weather fine & mild, transport animals much improved in condition, horse ambulance pinch pole or/places but transport animals evacuated are not replaced, otherwise ambulance again thoroughly refitted for a move forward.	RML

T.C. Hodgson Maj.
T.M.S.
O.C. Amballa Cav. Fd. Amb.

ORIGINAL

MEDICAL

Serial No. 5.

From 17th May to 30th June 1917.

War Diary from 1-5-17 to 31-5-17

VOLUME XXXIII

Ambala C.F.A. 4th Cav Divn

COMMITTEE FOR THE
MEDICAL HISTORY OF THE WAR
Date 27 JUL. 1917

E. C. Hodgson Maj.
I.M.S.

Place	Date	Hour	Summary of Events and Information	Remarks and references to Appendices
Sailly	1.5.17		The Inniskillings Regt reported that the billets we had occupied & which they had taken over had accumulations of manure which took two days to remove. Was able to show from Town Majors references that these were old manure heaps and that the accumulation was entirely exaggerated. It did not seem to have occured to the officer who made the report to enquire into the matter, the manure was withdrawn. 2/Lt Browne R.A.M.C. went on leave to England. We are admitting both British & Indians from the M.mr 13 de & admit cases from the whole division.	
	3.5.17		Inspected the sanitation of Sailon village which contains C.I.H., Fd H.2.H. A Battery with A.m.O. Col.H. was unable & asked consent to use of his reserve Co. Batt. to relieve the sergt to ensure any conditions (illegible) left by the previous troops. Wrote for 126 empty petrol tins for water for the three un-locoed to have one to be carried till water to the water tank when going for water would add considerably to the weight of the cart & it seems to me doubtful if cars	

WAR DIARY
or
INTELLIGENCE SUMMARY.

Army Form C. 2118.

(Erase heading not required.)

Instructions regarding War Diaries and Intelligence Summaries are contained in F. S. Regs., Part II. and the Staff Manual respectively. Title pages will be prepared in manuscript.

Place	Date	Hour	Summary of Events and Information	Remarks and references to Appendices
Sailon	3.5.17		Animals will be able after to pull the cart over bad ground. The animals are now fed out of hay nets & have a full ration. Feed any have quite recovered from their exposure a fortnight ago. The S.V.S. paid us a visit today & made the condition there ~~satisfactory~~. No goats or army in the division. The accommodation for both men & animals is far better & being more & more improved. The stock is good. Lt. Wheeler Wright returned from one month's leave today.	
	5.5.17		Have been overhauling all the wagons and replacing whenever & broken wheels, axles, etc. The cob's still heavy work to followers hydraulic steering damaged several wheels. Reinforces 250 blankets. Recommended the following N.C.O.'s for promotion. (1) Farrier (act. Corp.) Hennings to Corporal (2) Shoeing Smith Kane to Corporal (3) Dr. Wheeler Wright to act. corporal (4) L/c Cochrane to Corporal	

2353 Wt. W3544/1454 700,000 5/15 D. D. & L. A.D.S.S./Forms/C. 2118.

WAR DIARY
or
INTELLIGENCE SUMMARY.

(Erase heading not required.)

Army Form C. 2118

Place	Date	Hour	Summary of Events and Information	Remarks and references to Appendices
Santon	5.5.17		Lt Bruce to Yprecipal. Lt (Act. Capt) Mac Vicar to torpoual. This is the second time in accordance with 2nd A.S.C. orders I have recommended these men but although places for the promotions exist in the unit no promotions are made.	
	9.5.17		Held local sports for the unit today, in perfect weather after the showers of rain last night. There were a large number of entries for each event & also for the two rounders seven a side horses competition which showed plenty of keeness & the officers & men general has come off friendly in keenship to whom to award the prizes. The general result is the men was I consider excellent, leave for the men now starting to come in twenty months and no strong event to for amusements such as bands, theatrical companies, or cinemas, as in infantry units being at present available.	
	14.5.17		Evacuated all sick situation to No 1/3 C.C.S. Doullens in preparation of a move.	

Army Form C. 2118.

WAR DIARY
or
INTELLIGENCE SUMMARY.

(Erase heading not required.)

Instructions regarding War Diaries and Intelligence Summaries are contained in F.S. Regs., Part II. and the Staff Manual respectively. Title pages will be prepared in manuscript.

Place	Date	Hour	Summary of Events and Information	Remarks and references to Appendices
Hedly	15.5.17		Marched today from Sarton to here with the Whow Bde without any difficulty and are very comfortably billeted in the village. There were no accidents or sick to be dealt with on the march.	
Lavieville	16.5.17		Marched from Hedly to this village today, short march no trouble or accidents on the road, billets very rough, raining.	
Camped in quarry near Fricourt	17.5.17		Arrived here after long march over indifferent roads the tents & no accommodation. Large numbers of old German dug outs about. Splendid country for grazing, near the Somme. No difficulty about bathing or watering (Weather hot!) no wish to brigade. All men hard at work building huts from wood in dug outs.	
	19.5.17		Reported we had five Mule of James wheeler stretchers. One mule cut out into I.O.M. has returned only partly unroadic, nothing done to wheels or tops a part of pump missing	
	21.5.17		Sergt Mag Cooke proceeded on 14 days leave. Wrote to Staff Capt Whow Bde saying mail would be willing to take 16 dozen eggs a week if available. Provided	

WAR DIARY or INTELLIGENCE SUMMARY

Army Form C. 2118

Place	Date	Hour	Summary of Events and Information	Remarks and references to Appendices
Silchar	21.5.17		mgt fg to Rosiel & inspected A.D.S. of 59th & 59th Div. Fire also relay posts. Temperature in Yprès & aid post in Hangoard greatly was not suitable with any of them. A.D.S. dark. Bombing of operating room basement very bad severely death. Chosen but badly put together & to be no accommodation for either wounded officers or men if they were to be delivered quarters for medical officers in tent in the open & was no tiny hut. Can't have too neat latrines at any rate. Empty under cover no protection (wooden or personnel) will require enlarging work to put somewhat right. The hut has to be taken over by the units tomorrow & also another hospital being here in the trenches. Capt. Zoug & Capt. Bg. once detailed in charge of the S & D.S. with S.A. Brown Sergt. up. New huts & tents & R.C. Richardson is in charge of duties British personnel 16 at A.D.S. two mo. tpt. drivers at relay post & Indian 1 nt aux post & at relay post & 28 at A.D.S. One motor ambulance car remains at relay post & two at A.D.S.	

WAR DIARY or INTELLIGENCE SUMMARY

Army Form C. 2118

Place	Date	Hour	Summary of Events and Information	Remarks and references to Appendices
St Omer	22.5.17		Dr Mackay had to go to A.D.S. emplacem^t. Splitting Bougres which are still worth from probably [---] on any how. Coldcream was of no use there are five wells without water to wash or shave here in town use for any years and now constantly breaking down & giving out their time in the workshops. He sent location of emp^t in May 22.23/5/17 N.3.6.5.0	
	24.5.17		Am employing hospital with half an extra Sect with ambulance personnel but no float is supplied. The map references for the A.D.S. is 22.A.1/40,00. K.16.d.7.1. Requested him to obtain working pay for the Inkstone sergeant & six nursing orderlies of N° 2 Sec of S/Ambulance my belonging wait from D.A.D.9. Have telephoned orders what to do in case of a bombing attack from aeroplanes.	
	26.5.17		Open a hospital here. The arrangements now are that all sick wounded here & wounded at [---] the A.D.S. are not shown on the books of the Ambula (C.F.A.) but on that of the Divisional 2 C.F.A. because that is	

Army Form C. 2118

WAR DIARY
or
INTELLIGENCE SUMMARY.
(Erase heading not required.)

Instructions regarding War Diaries and Intelligence
Summaries are contained in F.S. Regs., Part II.
and the Staff Manual respectively. Title pages
will be prepared in manuscript.

Place	Date	Hour	Summary of Events and Information	Remarks and references to Appendices
S=Eloi Quarry	26.5.17		The Main Dressing Station. This causes a great increase of correspondence & difficulty in getting returns in time & correct.	
	27.5.17		He am made a report about evolution of old Sinclair motor ambulances which are constantly breaking down owing to weakness. This will spring. Number of wounded from division very small considering trenches are so bad.	
	29.5.17		One of the D Type ambulance cars broke its back wheel. They not being attached to the division. Borrowed one car from Snipe CE.F.A.	
	31.5.17		Again attention to shortage of straight animals drivers in ambulances here nearest reinforcements for some time. Personal being tried to improve hospital here and at D.S. at Renail this very depressed & often want blown walls will divide & busy to get own supposed own.	

J.C. Hodgson Major
O.C. Australia Cavalry Field Ambulance

— MEDICAL —

War Diary from 1/9 to 30/9

Volume XXXIV

1-Anzac Cav: Fd: Amb:

— ORIGINAL —

Army Form C. 2118.

WAR DIARY
or
INTELLIGENCE SUMMARY.
(Erase heading not required.)

Instructions regarding War Diaries and Intelligence Summaries are contained in F.S. Regs., Part II and the Staff Manual respectively. Title pages will be prepared in manuscript.

Place	Date	Hour	Summary of Events and Information	Remarks and references to Appendices
Roisel	1.6.17		The ambulance is divided into two sections, an advanced section at the advanced Dressing Station here & a line section at St Emilie in an old dressing station presently used by the Germans for same purpose. The A.D.S. carry deals with the wounded of the two left sectors of the division and the support & reserve also all the sick of corps & divisional troops in neighbourhood up to a track distance of nearly two miles. The that section deal with the remainder of the Brigade in the line who have been left to hang on to the lines. In the A.D.S. we are now rebuilding & the junction room and dressing room so that about the same time the cook-house dining room half the officers messing & a hygiene waggon (?) (2) The Wesham hut [sheds] was fitted up. Finally (3) they staff were comfortably housed. Sick promoted: British 2, 6 Indian 1, 3	

WAR DIARY
or
INTELLIGENCE SUMMARY.

(Erase heading not required.)

Army Form C. 2118.

Place	Date	Hour	Summary of Events and Information	Remarks and references to Appendices
Roisel	2/6/17		Ordered one horsed ambulance from tent section to march to with the Wharn Bde.	
			Sick & wounded passing through A.D.S. British Sick 4 Wounded 0	
			Indian 1 8	
			(Indian officer 0 1)	
	3/6/17		Obtained area iron beds from R.E.s for hospital at St Emut. Wrote to O.C. Supply Co. Workshops about oil burner getting no retorquent repaired.	
			British Sick 0 Wounded 3	
			Indian 7 0	
	4/6/17		The following reinforcements arrived:— Sick Wounded	
			British 4 0	Sp 29/404 Dr. Groves 18 y, cpl 56 H.T
			Indian 2 1	S/A 19/775 " Helton 9 H. " " "
				No 36739 " Zipper " " "
	5/6/17		Sgt Major Cright returned from leave in England & resuming no regimen.	
			British Sick 3× Wounded 0	
			Indian 1 0	
	6/6/17		In addition to admissions see 40 to 50 sick a day.	British Sick 4 Wounded 0
				Indian 3 0

Army Form C. 2118.

WAR DIARY
or
INTELLIGENCE SUMMARY.
(Erase heading not required.)

Instructions regarding War Diaries and Intelligence Summaries are contained in F. S. Regs., Part II. and the Staff Manual respectively. Title pages will be prepared in manuscript.

Place	Date	Hour	Summary of Events and Information	Remarks and references to Appendices
Roval	7.6.17		The village was heavily shelled with 5.9 & 8 inch German guns, most of the shells going to the other end of the village near the railway station. There seems to be coming a regular thing once or twice a week, but not usually so heavily. However it is very seldom anyone is hurt & wasted German ammunition. British Sick 10 Wounded 3 / Indians 4 0	
	8.6.17		British Sick 4 Wounded 3 / Indians 3 0	
	9.6.17		Aviator can't too badly needed to replace a leaking one wrote D.A.D.O.S. British Sick 2 Wounded 0 / Indians 1 0	
	10.6.17		Wrote about completing the inoculation of the D.G. & 44th Indian Bat. x includes one officer. British Sick 7x Wounded 1 / Indians 3 0	
	11.6.17		Received first intimation that brigade may possibly make an attack. Alterations here to be completed in a couple of days. x includes one officer. British Sick 6x Wounded 7 / Indians 3 4	

Army Form C. 2118.

WAR DIARY
or
INTELLIGENCE SUMMARY.

(Erase heading not required.)

Instructions regarding War Diaries and Intelligence Summaries are contained in F. S. Regs., Part II. and the Staff Manual respectively. Title pages will be prepared in manuscript.

Place	Date	Hour	Summary of Events and Information	Remarks and references to Appendices
Road	12.6.17		There is considerable irritation in front, weather fine & dry. British 5 sick 4* Indians 4 5	*Includes one officer
	13.6.17		Recommended that Sergt. Wood (in event to have an input for general service as he has a theorem of victims & constantly recurrent blistering pills & strongest order to send him to some I.B.D. I.R.S. British Sick 4* Indians 0 1	*Includes one officer "Ditto"
	14.6.17		Complained officially of the general input condition of the 5 Sirdiwan motors but C in C said it could be responsible for them working efficiently in coming action & begged they might be replaced by lorries accessible & fit to the work, the would be started for 12th Division front. British 4* Indians 2 8	*Includes one officer
	15.6.17		Started work in regimental aid post with Kahan under orders R.S. Sick 3* Indians 1 4	*Includes one officer

2353 Wt. W2544/1454 700,000 5/15 D. D. & L. A.D.S.S./Forms/C. 2118.

WAR DIARY or INTELLIGENCE SUMMARY

Army Form C. 2118.

Place	Date	Hour	Summary of Events and Information	Remarks and references to Appendices
Roisel	16.6.17		The arrangements with regard to the taking in of patients on A. & D. trains is as follows. There is one main dressing station for the two divisions of Indian cavalry. This is at "Berneo". There are two Advanced Dressing Stations, one at Roisel for the sector on the left, held by the 4th Cav. Div. & the other at Gouzeaucourt for the right sector, held by the 5th Cav. Div. which contains a brigade of Canadians. This A.D.S. draws also an advance Tpt of the 4th Cav. Div. but the greater number of casualties pass through the A.D.S. at Roisel because the right part of the line is on an average 600 yds to 1000 yds from the German line while on the left they are 300 yds to 400 yds only and in places are less than 100 yds apart. In addition to the main dressing stations of Berneo there is a Rest Camp at St Leger & Rest Camp at Doingt No. 36 & 39 (C.S.) at Tincourt & the two new C.C.S. at Peronne, La Chapelette, in addition there are two (C.S.) employed ^A at personnel in ordinary to which we are attached, for special C.C.S. for the 4th Army.	

Place	Date	Hour	Summary of Events and Information	Remarks and references to Appendices
Roisel	16.6.17		Self inflicted wounds and shell shock or N.Y.D. shall cases as they are now called. The arrangement is that neither the A.D.S. or the Rest Camp automatically show such admissions on their books and only the Corps Main Dressing Station does that. The Corps Main Dressing Stations are two one for the British Cav. Divisions the 2nd & 3rd on our left and the one at Beaume for both Indian & British patients of the 4 & 5th Indian Cav. Divisions. The Corps Main Dressing Station at Beaume is run by the 5th Div. Sanitary and Field Ambulance assisted by contingents from the 5th Div. Canadian Field Ambulance and the 4 & 5 Div. Sections Field Ambulance. The Corps Rest Station at St Emin is run by the 4 Div. Lucknow Cav. Field Ambulance assisted by a contingent from the Canadian C.F.A. The arrangement at the A.D.S. is that they change about every 12 days of personnel, that at Roisel two ambulances remains permanently in charge.	

WAR DIARY
or
INTELLIGENCE SUMMARY

Army Form C. 2118.

(Erase heading not required.)

Place	Date	Hour	Summary of Events and Information	Remarks and references to Appendices
Roisel	16.6.17		on the A & D. books. This arrangement of admitting only at the Main Dressing Station causes an excessive amount of writing to the subalterns in action, as practically they have to keep their A & D. book without numbering the cases or showing them officially & sending all the information each time to the Main Dressing Station in time for the wires & returns or otherwise great confusion is caused. The A.D.S. on supplies at Ambulances Collecting Post at Templeux where I am in charge of a day also. A very orderly & are stretcher bearers and another nine stretcher bearers under a rank at the Aid Post — in the quarry near Hargicourt. The wounded are brought down from this Aid Post to Templeux (a mile) on wheeled stretcher carriages by our bearers to the Amb. Collecting Post at Templeux, where in addition to the Indian personnel there is kept one light Ford ambulance & one large sunbeam ambulance with from drivers. From Templeux they are brought to the A.D.S. here in	

Place	Date	Hour	Summary of Events and Information	Remarks and references to Appendices
Road	16.6.17		Ten minutes along a very good road & there are numerous casualties an officer goes from the A.D.S. to the Collecting Post to dress any bad cases & any beginning to show signs of being infected etc. & to see there is no hitch. One very noticeable point has come out during the stay of the Indian Divisions in the trenches this time compared to the last term of duty as infantry in the trenches in September 1915 opposite Neuve Chapelle and that is as case of even suspicious wounds known (of being self inflicted) has occurred this time amongst Indians. Last time it was very much otherwise as a large percentage were then hit in the left fore arm & hand & were very suspicious in fact many personal opinions there was no doubt of foul play, now there has not been a single suspicious wound and the moral is shown by the spirit of the wounded passing through is a hundred times better. So a single case of shell shock among	

WAR DIARY
or
INTELLIGENCE SUMMARY

Army Form C. 2118.

Place	Date	Hour	Summary of Events and Information	Remarks and references to Appendices
Raval	16.6.17		Indians, and their whole bearing and morale was at least 100% better, great reviews and enthusiasm too keen & is being shown, inspite of the fact that whether nowadays is worth much heavier casualties & much heavier and more contagious fire. Indians are from trenches & almost unknown. Casualties: British 3 / 3, Indians 1 / 0. The cash shown here are from trial antimonous to Italians etc not in the line	
	17.6.17		Noticed Anopheles mosquitos here & at St Chirot particularly in the Somme Valley. 7 am appeared to be on anopheles distribution but without a microscope it is impossible to say. The weather appears warm enough for malaria the mosquitos parasite in the mosquito but fortunately there do not appear to be scarcely any cases of genuine malaria though one Indian passed through here with a splenic malaria above the ribs and referring to the quality of Quinine Bisque available. Casualties: British 3* / 1, Indians 5 / 7. *includes one officer. Wounded	

WAR DIARY
or
INTELLIGENCE SUMMARY

Army Form C. 2118.

Place	Date	Hour	Summary of Events and Information	Remarks and references to Appendices
Rawal	18.6.17		The ambulance has been short of water to it from the beginning of our work in the trenches owing to me of our a.v.s. ($\frac{7}{8}$ to Hay orders) to the forward brigade headquarters by the norm and was not returned even after one of our water carts broke down and the hospital & units had to make their arrangements to cook with tea etc.	
	19.6.17		2nd Bartley was transferred to the Sialkot C.I.H. yesterday.	
			Am posting with this my relations of local units	
				Wounded
			British	0
			Indians 8	0
			British	1
			Indians 7+	2
		20.6.17	British 6+	0 Includes one officer
			Indians 4	0
			Recommended Wheeler Wright for promotion to Corporal & again with pay. He has given up all trunk work a completely different man.	

WAR DIARY
or
INTELLIGENCE SUMMARY.

(Erase heading not required.)

Army Form C. 2118.

Place	Date	Hour	Summary of Events and Information	Remarks and references to Appendices
Rizal	20.6.17		Recommended L/Cpl. W. Stear to be promoted A/Sgt in place of Sergt. Wood promoted to Stores & St Lankment to be promoted L/Cpl in place of W. Stear	
			Sick Wounded	
	21.6.17		British 1 0	
			Indians 0 4	
	22.6.17		British 2 4	
			Indians 0 0	
			Am now building a new cook house, store room & etc to supply. Have every thing arranged for dealing with 400 wounded in 24 hours. Typ cases are again increasing (?) Persons	
	23.6.17		Sick Wounded	
			British 4 0	
			Indians 1 1	
	24.6.17		British 9 1	
			Indians 0 0	
	25.6.17		British 4 0	
			Indians 2 1	

WAR DIARY or INTELLIGENCE SUMMARY

Army Form C. 2118.

Place	Date	Hour	Summary of Events and Information	Remarks and references to Appendices
Roiral	25.6.17		Have arranged for all slightly wounded to be taken next day or the both at A.D.S. and at Tampleux existing post. Mumps has broken out amongst the Indian Tendering to turn from Marseilles. Expurgation & daily examination is being carried out.	
	26.6.17		Sick / Wounded British 2 / 0 Indians 1 / 1	
	27.6.17		British 5 / 0 Indians 1 / 1	
	28.6.17		British 3 / 2* *including one officer Indians 2 / 8	
	29.6.17		There was heavy firing last night & Roiral came in for a share in the morning, no one however hit Sick / Wounded British 3 / 1 Indians 1 / 2* 2* includes one officer British 3 / — Indians 2 / 8	

R.C. Hodgson, Maj.
O.C. Ambulance I.F.A.

M — MEDICAL —

— DUPLICATE —

Serial No. 5

War Diary from 1/7 to 31/7/17

Volume xxxv.

Ambala Cav Fd Amb

COMMITTEE FOR THE
MEDICAL HISTORY OF THE WAR
Date 16 OCT. 1917

T. C. Hodgson Maj. I.M.S.
O.C. Ambala C.F.A.

Army Form C. 2118.

WAR DIARY
or
INTELLIGENCE SUMMARY.
(Erase heading not required.)

Place	Date	Hour	Summary of Events and Information	Remarks and references to Appendices
Road	1.7.17		Very quiet day on front. Am making arrangements for the road tomorrow. At the A.D.S. here have built a circular road about 250 yards long and looked it from the road so that the motor ambulances bringing back wounded can turn off the road, unload the wounded (& the two huts & the officers wounded along without delay to a point further up where from a tent they can draw fresh stretchers & blankets and then myself up to the places allotted to them to wait for the wounded after they have been dressed. The wounded on arrival are at once separated into lying cases and walking cases. The lying cases are taken immediately to the waiting room adjoining the operating theatre from these they are taken on to the two operating tables where two medical officers assisted by two nursing orderlies and two to do orderlies deal with the cases. One nursing orderly to see in charge of the sterilising room next door & supplies sterilized dressing, towels, hot water et	

Place	Date	Hour	Summary of Events and Information	Remarks and references to Appendices
Road	9.1.17		From there the wounded are to be taken & put into the cars waiting at the door & sent to the C.C.S., if severely wounded, at Incourt, or to the Main Dressing Station at Berne. If the wounded have penetrating wounds of the abdomen or severe injuries to the head arrangement has been made that I shall send notice from the Ambulance Collecting Station at Templeuve and the patients shall be seen by one of the M.O.'s in the car who will have particulars taken by the S.A. Surgeon & send on the cases without delay for immediate operation at the C.C.S. without disturbing the patients. If the patients arriving # on after dressing are found too bad to take on they are to be given saline infusions & stimulants and placed in one of the adjacent huts where they can be watched and sent on as soon as they show signs of recovery from shock. Walking wounded are attended to in the second hut which has been arranged so that on arrival the patients sit on	

Army Form C. 2118.

WAR DIARY
or
INTELLIGENCE SUMMARY.
(Erase heading not required.)

Instructions regarding War Diaries and Intelligence Summaries are contained in F. S. Regs. Part II. and the Staff Manual respectively. Title pages will be prepared in manuscript.

Place	Date	Hour	Summary of Events and Information	Remarks and references to Appendices
Roisel	1.7.17		branches and have their dressings removed by batmen who have been trained in the work and then move up to where the medical officer examines them and orders treatment they are then dressed by the sub-assistant surgeon, a nursing orderly & three ward boy/dressers. They are then given anti tetanus by an M.O. (extra one if available in village) and sent out to tents where the padres give them hot drinks, soup, sandwiches & the Staff Sergeant sends (them on by the working motors to the main dressing station at Berne. Particulars & cards are made out by the clerk & orderly detailed) the M.O.s filling in notes. The motor sergeant arranges that on arrival of one car with wounded from the collecting station another goes up at once and that order & discipline is kept among the cars. Seven motor ambulances are kept going, three at the collecting post and four at the A.D.S., more can be obtained from Main dressing station if required and three horse ambulances are kept	

Place	Date	Hour	Summary of Events and Information	Remarks and references to Appendices
Noral	1.7.17		ready with the horses with their harness on in stables in case they are required farther forward. To prevent patients being dressed unnecessarily of the arrangements have been made that no two will be sent if cases do not require dressing again for some hours. At the Collecting Post I have arranged that I will see all cases passing through, only redress those requiring it though, readjust tourniquets, splints etc. & give hot drinks to those fit for them, divide up wounded into (1) cases direct to C.C.S. (2) lying cases (3) sitting cases, & see wounded transferred from horse ambulances, wheeled ambulances, or walking cases into motor ambulances etc. My staff will consist of myself, two Indian ward orderlies, a batman to prepare tea, a Dufadar to have charge of & replace stretchers & the carrying of blankets & stretchers strictly to deal with those sent with patients & a motor transport corporal with ears the reg ulating of any horse ambulances, wheeled ambulances, stretchers etc.	

WAR DIARY
or
INTELLIGENCE SUMMARY.

(Erase heading not required.)

Army Form C. 2118.

Place	Date	Hour	Summary of Events and Information	Remarks and references to Appendices
Rouzih	1.7.17		The arrangement of M.O.s & tent sections of ambulance & transport dealing with each of brigade in bank area. Capt Rennie, Lt Mackay & Lt Kirshner Macyth at A.D.S. with two S.A.S., four nursing orderlies & two ward orderlies. Sergeant Major, 3 Staff Sergeants, 3 Motor Sergeants all ambulance collecting part myself, two wardorderlies, & mob corporal & compliment of bearers at this post at the rear work of the A.B.C. & storing working under Capt Pomfrey T.M.S. in charge of the emergency dress party. Dr Milligan proceeded on leave to H.K. Admissions to A.D.S. Sick Wounded British 4 — Indian 3 —	
	2.7.17		All preparations for raid completed and worked smoothly. The number of wounded dealt with during the day being 40 of whom 33 were British & 7 Indians only 29 (all British) went	

Army Form C. 2118.

WAR DIARY
or
INTELLIGENCE SUMMARY.
(Erase heading not required.)

Instructions regarding War Diaries and Intelligence Summaries are contained in F. S. Regs., Part II. and the Staff Manual respectively. Title pages will be prepared in manuscript.

Place	Date	Hour	Summary of Events and Information	Remarks and references to Appendices
Raval	2.7.17		actually wounded in the raid). Two died at the A.D.S. one British & one Indian. Everyone worked well, especially Capt. Benner R.A.M.C. & nursing orderlies Rowlands & Baxter. Corpl. Easterbrook also did remarkably well. All wounded in raid with the exception of four were hit with fragments of bomb whether our own or of Germans it is impossible to say, two apparent but quite a shell one a rifleman from an captain men of explosive series, & one for bomb & also slight bayonet wound accidental from one of the own men. Eleven men unwounded Prisoners taken & the genl. opinion is not 60 killed in trenches or dug outs	
	3.7.17		Sick Wounded British 4 4 Indian 0 1 British 18 0 Indian 2 2	
	4.7.17			
	5.7.17		Received orders to open A. & D. Books from noon today	

WAR DIARY
or
INTELLIGENCE SUMMARY.
(Erase heading not required.)

Army Form C. 2118.

Place	Date	Hour	Summary of Events and Information	Remarks and references to Appendices
Rinal	5/7/17		1 officer and 12 men of the 103rd Field Ambulance arrived to take over but we are not to hand over till the 10th (Thornville)	
			Sick	
			British 2	
			Indians 2	
			British 0	
			Indians 3	
	6/7/17		British 2 1	Two wounded men this night
			Indians 0 1	enquiry on found but on Inspection by
	7/7/17		British 2 0	the man died of shock.
			Indians 0 0	S.A.S. Dettan Singh sent to St Priest.
	8/7/17		A very quiet day on front, weather cold & rainy	
			A. & D. tooks again ordered to be closed at Fresnilly today.	
			British 9 0	3 British officers rec'd, one wounded
			Indians 1 6	1 Indian Officer wounded
	9/7/17		So British 10 2	
			Indians 1 0	
			There has been heavy shelling on the front but few casualties	

Army Form C. 2118.

WAR DIARY
or
INTELLIGENCE SUMMARY.
(Erase heading not required.)

Place	Date	Hour	Summary of Events and Information	Remarks and references to Appendices
St Omer	10.7.17		Marched from Advanced Dressing Station at Reveil to St Omer after handing over A.D.S. & Collecting Post etc. to 103rd Infantry Field Ambulance, the whole of our division being first clear of the line, arriving here at 12 A.M. King's hospital here & found S.A.K.D. Bootys are taking in patients from both Sialkot & Lucknow Bolea. Applied for another half eighteen Hut as accommodation for Indians not sufficient.	
	12.7.17		Dr Caleb went on special leave to England.	
	14.7.17		The following staff was ordered to proceed (near strips to look after sick of coolie corps & be attached to VIIth Corps. S.A.S. Dhun Roy, o/No 5 22 Ward orderly Fazal Ahmed o/No 5141 Bisgut Krishna, No 278 Bhisti Mohammed Din, No 283 Sweeper Kalhu. This will leave us very short in Indian medical personnel.	
	15.7.17		Dr Hilton proceeded on special leave. Pte Jones returned to 6 (?) Travelling Dys. A/Serjt Stevens C.A.S.C., A.T. rejoined from Base, te Havre.	

WAR DIARY or INTELLIGENCE SUMMARY

Army Form C. 2118.

Place	Date	Hour	Summary of Events and Information	Remarks and references to Appendices
	18/7/17		Had some suggestion of cerebro spinal meningitis which I sent in to special C.O.S. & took all precautions. Received information from A.D.M.S. that not more tents could be given for the sick.	
	19/7/17		2/Lt. 17422 Rennie Gofney evacuated to Kinghorn C.C.S. for chronic indigestion. Dr. Mulligan returned from leave.	
	20/7/17		Dr. Light proceeded on leave to U.K. One have evacuated to hosp. yesterday for mumps. Another during boys tried to prevent escape. He was tried to + severely injured himself last night. Returned 3 medical comfort books to me Dressing Hosp. 504 M.B.D.	
	22/7/17		Had two cases ambulatory wire malaria. Made filling & sent them to Mustaphajit. Received reply Cpl. who afraid case negative. Repts (a) Sanit. Off. 2/Lt 32.79 Sutler pthmus. 36 Jacobs Home sent in by 25 forbes G.M.S. (2C) suffering from eczema, foul urinaceo. [?] over 100 maggots to 5.4 D.M.S. sent in tent on 20 July. Wrote about changing Sergt. Handley who is not up to running with transport.	

WAR DIARY
or
INTELLIGENCE SUMMARY.
(Erase heading not required.)

Army Form C. 2118.

Place	Date	Hour	Summary of Events and Information	Remarks and references to Appendices
Sialkot	25/7/17		Dt Everett Dt Mutlinden proceeded on leave to U.K. The Divisional Horse show examined today we showed two horses ambulances with which we won 1st & 3rd prize. Sialkot winning 2nd prize, also a humbered G.S. wagon with 6 mules but did not even with that. Corp. Wheeler Wright Sergt. Major Cooke & Sergt. Mitchell were largely responsible for the excellent condition in which all the wagons were turned out. The event amplified a keen rivalry & so tucked all ranks. The officers horse at a jump & horse fell CE Yorks fell with his horse at a jump & horse fell on him breaking his pelvis near the symphisis and tearing the urethra. He was at once sent on to the C.C.S. for operation. Bearer Mahomed Azim, M Gigri Shumbos & Shick Abdul Rahman proceeded on leave to U.K.	
	26/7/17		Farrier Corp. Hemmings proceeded on leave to U.K. The Horse show was continued & was a great success. No one injured severely today. Saddler Corp. Gruer proceeded on leave to U.K.	

Army Form C. 2118.

WAR DIARY
or
INTELLIGENCE SUMMARY.

(Erase heading not required.)

Instructions regarding War Diaries and Intelligence Summaries are contained in F. S. Regs., Part II. and the Staff Manual respectively. Title pages will be prepared in manuscript.

Place	Date	Hour	Summary of Events and Information	Remarks and references to Appendices
S.E. of Chocques	29.7.19		Sergt Hindley A.S.C. sent to Gosspin C.I.of Omniforthing Brigade has this men, over a Commiforthing places on main Somme Rd. The amount of sickness among Indian units is infuriating but there is a certain amount of P.U.O. & diarrhoea among Portuguese which I put down to chinese meet.	
	31.7.19		Lt Hope & Pte Wainthorpe invalided on leave to U.K. Pte F. Wheeler to diminishing days joined unit.	

F.C. Hodgson Major
f. m. S.
O.C. Ambulance C.I.H.

MEDICAL

Serial No. 5.

ORIGINAL

Aug '17

War Diary from 1/7 to 31/7.

Volume XXXVI.

1- Imbala Cav. Fd. 1-Imp

COMMITTEE FOR THE
MEDICAL HISTORY OF THE WAR
Date 16 OCT 1917

Army Form C. 2118.

WAR DIARY
or
INTELLIGENCE SUMMARY.

(Erase heading not required.)

Instructions regarding War Diaries and Intelligence Summaries are contained in F.S. Regs., Part II. and the Staff Manual respectively. Title pages will be prepared in manuscript.

Place	Date	Hour	Summary of Events and Information	Remarks and references to Appendices
St Christ	1.8.17		The Hospital Hut was leaking badly so have written for tarred felt to completely recover the whole building as it is useless patching. Recommended Nos 785, 8 Coy & 13.C. & Sgt Martin be promoted (?) 2nd Cpl. Am building brigade half water bath near river but think the site chosen by the Engineers is very unhealthy & likely to be troublesome in wet weather. Sgt Mc Ivor & Dr Bragg proceeded on 10 days leave to the U.K.	
	3.8.17		There has been a certain amount of desertion among the Labour Battalion which I put down to the men suffering from non-delivery of water rations. The O.C. has been warned to stop these P.U.O. cases as are frequent among British & may be common among Indians. Can this be due to the large proportion of time men are being sent in the line rations? Ptes Gowling, Dr Manson & Brown proceeded on 10 days leave to the U.K.	
	5.8.17		Forwarded letter from Lt Walsh re Meeting of Army Commission ??	

WAR DIARY
or
INTELLIGENCE SUMMARY.
(Erase heading not required.)

Army Form C. 2118.

Place	Date	Hour	Summary of Events and Information	Remarks and references to Appendices
St Chud	3.8.17		his contract on 3rd September. Wrote again to Field Disbursing Officer I.E.F.A. asking for a statement of accounts of Indians with the unit. It is scandal that during 3 years service no single statement of accounts of any Indian has been sent this unit in spite of repeated requests by the previous O.C. & myself. 2nd Krishna Murthy proceeded on 10 days leave to the U.K.	
Fournes	7.8.17		Marched here yesterday and took over hospital etc. Build by the Sirhid C.F.A. at once and collecting from the Mhow 15 the Lucknow C.F.A. taking over from us and the Sealkot C.F.A. taking over the divisional rest station from the Lucknow C.F.A. Have to make hospital accommodation here for 25 horse lines etc mainly & hospital huts which will necessitate us retaining this new open having first completed the one at Sailly. There is no officers mess. We are preparing one having wood & the office needs rebuilding. Mosquitoes flies too annoying and are still very numerous.	

WAR DIARY
or
INTELLIGENCE SUMMARY.

Army Form C. 2118.

Place	Date	Hour	Summary of Events and Information	Remarks and references to Appendices
Fauquex	8.8.17		Was inspected by the D.M.S. 3rd Army Surgeon General Murray. Having this morning accompanied by the A/D.M.S. 4.D. He first inspected all the A.P.C. men. Then the Motor men, wagons & their engines, then the motor transport, marching order horses & finally the hospital. He having took leave & departing leaving he congratulated me on the turn out which he said was "all very good indeed".	
			Dr Sommert & Powell proceeded on 10 days leave to the U.K. Corpl. Hemmings returned from leave. Motor Cyclist Bryett met with a severe accident near Frevent & has been brought in with a paralysed muscaelo spinarmajor. The accident was not due to anyones carelessness.	
	10.8.17		Pte Dyke & Dr Duffy proceeded on 10 days leave to the U.K.	
	12.8.17		Dr Maskery proceeded on 10 days leave to the U.K. Pte Rowlands attended a gas course at the division.	

Army Form C. 2118.

WAR DIARY
or
INTELLIGENCE SUMMARY.
(Erase heading not required.)

Place	Date	Hour	Summary of Events and Information	Remarks and references to Appendices
Lourpres	14.8.17		Sergt. McEwan & Pt. Bragg have returned from leave. Examined Pte Cantrell 6 to 7 Dys. for mental trouble and sent him to the mental specialist of 3 Canadian Stat. Hospital Boulogne. He killed a comrade with a bayonet on way slightest provocation. Lt Benner went up for one day to look after the Minor dismount Batt. & is to be relieved by 2/Lt Merrin Merrin on his return from leave.	
	17.8.17		2/Lt Merrithy returned from leave & relieves Lt Benner. Pte Hazlewood & Dr Kielly proceeds on 10 days leave to U.K.	
	18.8.17		Ptes. Wood & Johnson & Dr Radcliffe proceed on 10 days leave to the U.K. Attended a lecture on the new German Mustard gas on dichlordiethyl, collecting material for building an Officers mess on the tent Clarke.	
	20.8.17		2/Lt Merrithy returned from Minor dismount Bathe yesterday & proceeded	

A 5834 Wt.W4973/M687 750,000 8/16 D. D. & L. Ltd. Forms/C.2118/13.

WAR DIARY
or
INTELLIGENCE SUMMARY.

(Erase heading not required.)

Army Form C. 2118.

Place	Date	Hour	Summary of Events and Information	Remarks and references to Appendices
Gonrehu	21.8.17		Today I jointly to be attached to the 10th & 11th to look after hours(?) Lr? & wounded of the division in the line. 3rd Grade f.S. Sanders Led. Lt. joins applied for promise 6.6.1 pm.	
	22.8.17		Lw Sumner v. Ewell returned from leave pm.	
	25.8.17		Major E.L.L. Logan pvt. proceeds on one month's special leave to England. Lt. Field Ambulance S.M.O. Kinlet to Cuiulham Camp. Special proceeds to Lualaba for two days leave pm.	
	24.8.17 25.8.17		Capt. H.S. Ingram R.A.M.C attends Army Gas school at H.Q. 2nd Army pm. Capt. H.S. Ingram attends Army Gas lecture at H.Q. 2nd Army. Lieut Jack Smith Hart joined 5.10. pm. G. Sinclair proceeds to Calais for Coast leave rear 5.10. pm.	
	26.8.17		G. Ewart CRR proceeds to Calais to attend Course Ranark poles Practice on 15th LR. A&C Check return. Attend from leave to H.R. pm.	
	27.8.17		Capt. Henry R.A.M.C. attend F.A.D. Gas Lecture at H.Q. 2nd A Corps pm. Lieut Maclay R.A.M.C. returns from 4 days leave to the U.K. CSM Baker Whis the Unit. pm	

WAR DIARY
or
INTELLIGENCE SUMMARY

Army Form C. 2118.

Place	Date	Hour	Summary of Events and Information	Remarks and references to Appendices
Ferozepur	28/8/17		Inspected 180 men 1, 3 Lahore Cay. not turned fully 40 I.P. from Lucknow B troop. Capt Bonner and Lt Mackay attended several gun lectures of Brig H.Q. A. Kahar Zorze was exponentiated to Intervene C.O.'s from Ambala ejtra. arrived with party at Picadilly Row.	
	29/8/17		Inspected 100 men of 34 Lahore Cay. for change of category where necessary. Ptes Johnson & McNutt and Radcliffe A&C HT returned from leave to U.K. One N.C.O. Ward A.S.C. under orders from S.O.Q. Bom. 4/26/5/17 left this depot to the O.C. A.S.C. 3rd Cav. Div. Pune.	
	30/8/17			
	31/8/17		Daff. Shen Singh attended gym lecture at B'Hrs. Pune.	
	19th		D/H. Shen Singh attended several gym lectures at O.H.Q. Pune.	

MEDICAL

Serial No. 5

COMMITTEE FOR THE
MEDICAL HISTORY OF THE WAR
Date 12 DEC. 1917

R.C. Hodgson
Major

WAR DIARY from 1/9/17 to 30/9/17

VOLUME XXXVII

AMBALA CAV: FLD: AMBULANCE

ORIGINAL
Sept. 1917

WAR DIARY
or
INTELLIGENCE SUMMARY.

(Erase heading not required.)

Army Form C. 2118.

Place	Date	Hour	Summary of Events and Information	Remarks and references to Appendices
FOURVES	Sept 1917 1st		Jem/Shu Singh attended third gas lecture at 9HQ here.	
	2nd		Lieut Mullis evacuated to Lucknow CCS with debility. S/Sgt Rowland F.P.S.W. went on 10 days leave to England. H. Parsons returned from 10 days leave.	
	3rd		Apo Guim Kahan of advanced section were relieved by a similar number from here. The warrant officers and Serjts were also relieved. Sgt Knighsmith RE was under orders from W.O. (letter 121/K/479. A.M.D.I of 29/8/17 received under O.O Nos 4093 4/3/9/17) was recalled from the advanced section, POEVILLY in order to return to England. He was replaced by Sgt Shackney RAMC. P/Cpl Wilson RE returning from leave. Run	
	4th		Lieut Knighsmith left the unit this evening to return to England. Run	
	5th		Serjt Mitchel returned from leave to England.	
	6th		Lieut J.R.S. Mackay rejoined this unit from the 104th Field Ambulance. Captain RM Lervy left for 10 days leave to Great Britain. OVD	

Army Form C. 2118.

WAR DIARY
or
INTELLIGENCE SUMMARY.
(Erase heading not required.)

Instructions regarding War Diaries and Intelligence Summaries are contained in F. S. Regs., Part II. and the Staff Manual respectively. Title pages will be prepared in manuscript.

Place	Date	Hour	Summary of Events and Information	Remarks and references to Appendices
	6		The party which were sent to compete in the Corps Horse Show near Pt. Rob returned today. They did not get a prize as the horses were said to be too large/heavy for the work. Gnrs. Pte Cleveland & Stockley returned from leave.	
	7		R.A.D.M.S. visited the Ambulance & inspected new Officers mess.	AMB
	8		Drivers Cleveland & Stockley arrived from leave.	AMB
	9		Driver Davis arrived from leave.	AMB
	10		Private Briggs wheeler proceeded on leave.	AMB
	11		Nothing to note.	AMB
	12		Private Barker was given 14 days F.P. No 1 for an offence dated 9/5/17.	AMB
	13		Private Briggs proceeded on leave & No 3655 Bearer FAZAL ELAHI No 3 Sqn. A.B.C. was transferred to Lucknow C.F.A.	AMB
	14		Nothing to note. A.D.M.S. 4 Cav. Div. visited the unit and saw selected sites for winter quarters. He also inspected the present quarters of the whole of the personnel.	AMB
	15		The Ambala C.F.A Concert party gave a very successful concert at ATHIES. The G.O.C. Brigade was present. Driver Bunce reported his arrival from the 3rd Army School of Cookery.	AMB
	16		Lance Corpl. Rowlands reported his arrival from leave.	AMB

Army Form C. 2118.

WAR DIARY
or
INTELLIGENCE SUMMARY.
(Erase heading not required).

Instructions regarding War Diaries and Intelligence Summaries are contained in F. S. Regs., Part II. and the Staff Manual respectively. Title pages will be prepared in manuscript.

Place	Date	Hour	Summary of Events and Information	Remarks and references to Appendices
	16th		No 4761 A.H.C. Cook BABU LAL & No 8972 Ward Servant AHURSAID ALI reported their arrival and were taken on the strength of the unit. AMB	
	17th		Driver Tyler, Billings & Jones returned from leave last night	
	18		Capt. A.J. Bonner proceeded on leave this morning. No. 4761 S.A. Cook Babu Lal proceeded to Lucknow Sta. for duty.	
	19th		Driver Lipot & Rondel with Rubbred G.S. Waggon proceeded to-day to report R & C to Indian Pioneer Battalion for temporary duty.	
	20th		S.Q.S. Dixon Smith and Befadas Shew Singh attended the presentation Chilton Punjab ceremony with of the Polo Tournament medals at Lucknow. Shew Singh were photographed at Headquarters.	
			1 Ward Orderly, 1 L/Naik and 4 Bearers and 1 Sweeper proceeded to-day for the 104th Field Ambulance to relieve the party at present there the Polo party arrived here on the same evening.	
	21st		No LKO/4765 Costo Lachman A.H.C. proceeded to-day to depart R.A.O.C. Lucknow S.Q. in place of No. 4761 Cook Babu Lal 81T who had been sent by mistake.	
			Capt. S.H.L. ARCHER R.A.V.C reported to-day for duty.	
	22nd		Capt. R.M. LANG reported his arrival from leave this evening. Gre G.S. Waggon 1 English speaking N.C.O. and 11 other ranks are going daily to the Mairie, Athies, commencing to-day, to clean area for Headquarters Coy.	

WAR DIARY
or
INTELLIGENCE SUMMARY.

Army Form C. 2118.

Place	Date	Hour	Summary of Events and Information	Remarks and references to Appendices
FOURDRES	23/9/17		Pte Craig 9th K.D.G. reported his arrival from 10 days leave to U.K. A.D.M.S. visited the unit. Maj. E.C. Hodgson RAMC reported his arrival from one month leave to U.K. and took over command of the unit. Corpl./Wheeler Wright A.S.C. reported hurt for duty. According to Div.Order M3724 2/11/15/17 he should have arrived in the evening of the 20th But Pte Wheeler 6 hours later reported his arrival from 10 days leave to U.K. RAMC	
	24.9.17		No 17489 Bearer Belair 1/2-7 Comp. A.B.C. reported his arrival for duty with this unit from Lushnow C.F.A. Saw A.D.M.S. and promised to try and arrange to get Mhow Bde HQ & Ambulances completed as regard their entire group inoculation as soon as possible. 50%	
	25.9.17		Dr Rich A.S.C. sent dental centre Fromure today & was detained. Shoeing Smith J.Coney joined unit in place of Shoeing Smith Ward (promoted) to another unit, from Area Horse Camp. The shrings recently issued from the ordnance dep. at base for the	

WAR DIARY
or
INTELLIGENCE SUMMARY.

Army Form C. 2118.

Place	Date	Hour	Summary of Events and Information	Remarks and references to Appendices
Fouquereuil	25.9.17		Wagon Ambulance Light Mark I, as side springs were found to have been wrongly put together, the stop leaf at the rear and having been reversed causing the roller to jar on the stop at once when even a single patient got in. These were taken off any reversed and are now quite satisfactory. 2nd Lt. Crossland R.A.S.C. M.T. was ordered to rush north 16/12 Boils to Div. Rest Station (Sialkot C.F.A.) on the 22nd Sept M/17 spoke to Capt. Keane R. at M.C. who is looking after 2nd Pioneer Batt. to have a regular weekly inspection of that unit as practically all Indian cases of scabies were coming from that unit. Spoke to 3rd Indian cav. Bde. on the 21st Sam Sf (Ers. author of our ambulance as re complete supplies we thought to ...	
	26.9.17		...	

WAR DIARY
or
INTELLIGENCE SUMMARY.

(Erase heading not required.)

Army Form C. 2118.

Place	Date	Hour	Summary of Events and Information	Remarks and references to Appendices
Fouquieres	27/9/17		Pte Short departed on leave & Pte Briggs returned from leave. Pte Briggs stated that the cause of his not returning to the unit on the day expected was that he had just been sent by R.T.O. Boulogne to Bethune.	
	28/9/17		Major Moore of 35th C.T.H. was evacuated (W) to ap 55 C.C.S. suffering from neuritis. Sergt Stevens A.S.C.A.T. & Pte Robertson R.A.M.C. started for Boulogne their leave starting on 28th. Forwarded correspondence with regard to the promotion of 2nd Gnde H.S.K. Baron Pershad to asst. 1st gnde to D.A.G. W.52, Base. 2t Chittenden J.W. A.S.C. H.T. proceeded on 12.27.9.1.7 High to Abbeville for one months course of instruction at F.B. cmt.	

WAR DIARY
INTELLIGENCE SUMMARY

Army Form C.2118.

Place	Date	Hour	Summary of Events and Information	Remarks and references to Appendices
Jhansi	29.9.17		Went up to Mhow Bde H.2 & spoke to the men of H.2 who had refused to be inoculated against Enteric & persuaded all except four old offenders to be done & with Capt Stoker maneuvered them on the spot. Proceed to Red Cross Stores at Saugnies and obtained a supply of pyjamas for the hospital. Was not able to obtain from Godsteads with the Q general indent signed by A.D.M.S. Dr Crossland was evacuated to J/2 5.5 C.C.S. on 27=x has been struck off our lists.	
	30.9.17		Weather for the last 10 days has been superb, most days beautiful sunshine but already cold(s) at night. It should be noisy nights still present but not active. First frost met(s) last night 1st grade H.S.K. Brohn Prahar transferred to Lucknow C.F.A. he has been an unsatisfactory workman & does not get on with others taking a British King. General Skid King invalided direct to 31.H. General Boulogne yesterday afternoon	

R.C. Ho Ayson Major I.M.S.
O.C. Ambala C.F.A.

Medical.

War Diary from 1/10/17 to 31/10/17

Vol. XXXVIII.

Ambala Cav. Fd. Amb.

COMMITTEE FOR THE
MEDICAL HISTORY OF THE WAR
Date 8 FEB. 1918

T.C. Hodgson
O.C. Ambala Cav. Fd. Amb.
I.M.S.

Original

AMBALA CAVALRY
FIELD AMBULANCE
No.
Date

WAR DIARY or INTELLIGENCE SUMMARY.

Army Form C. 2118.

Place	Date	Hour	Summary of Events and Information	Remarks and references to Appendices
TOURQUES	1/10/17		Capt. Bennee R.A.M.C. reported his arrival from ten days leave in England on 30.9.17. Sgt. Stackley returned from duty with the 4th Cav. dismounted brigade with his water cart & pair of mules.	
	2/10/17		Motor cycle E27 was sent in to workshops for repair this morning and at D.M.S. applied for for return of E28 which he has had on duty with him since 21st July. Weather remaining beautifully fine but cold at night. Held meeting yesterday to consider the question of starting a units canteen. Present S-M Winsbury, Sergt. Maj. Cooke, Sergt. Watherup, Corpl. Coulsbrook, Corpl. Rowlands, & S. Bragg. Decided to open both a dry & wet canteen in one of the old Cmte. Committees. Sgt. Maj. Cooke, Sgt. Watherup, Sgt. Rowlands, the latter being excused other duties at present to act as salesman. Sgt. Watherup kindly offering to do the accounts. The small committee to report to the above mention main committee once a week. The following men rejoined from the 104th Field Ambulance at Kneully where they had been looking after the sick and wounded of the 4th Cav. dismounted Brigade	

Army Form C. 2118.

WAR DIARY
or
INTELLIGENCE SUMMARY.

(Erase heading not required.)

Place	Date	Hour	Summary of Events and Information	Remarks and references to Appendices
Fouquières	2.10.17		who were holding a part of the line in front of Le Verguier. Ward Orderly at 1587 Bhura Rawat Sepoy No. 9131 Amrath A.B.C. " 17479 Gopal Singh " " " 7434 Ganga " " " 13044 Mohomedazim " " " 3957 Karam Khan " " " 3567 Kurra Sweeper	
	3.10.17		Dr. Beale A.S.C., H.I. rejoined from dental centre Pernes. Corpl. Wheeler Wright rep returned to Div. H.2. this morning.	
	4.10.17		Noted that Corpl. Wheeler Wright is working now in Attics and not on wagons in workshops, and the hospitals hide requires extensive alterations to make it habitable in winter. Will apply for his return. The following A.B.C. men returned from Div. H.Q. from detached duties under A.D.M.S. No. 5197 Beaner Tgairon " 5200 " Bhoora " 5387 " Motee	

Army Form C. 2118.

WAR DIARY
or
INTELLIGENCE SUMMARY.
(Erase heading not required.)

Instructions regarding War Diaries and Intelligence Summaries are contained in F. S. Regs., Part II. and the Staff Manual respectively. Title pages will be prepared in manuscript.

Place	Date	Hour	Summary of Events and Information	Remarks and references to Appendices
Fouquereuil	5.10.17		Lieutenant A.S. General I.M.S. (T.C.) reported his arrival yesterday and was taken on the strength of the unit. He arrived without any bedding or personal equipment having been informed at the India Office he would not require it. Capt. Archer R.A.M.C. (T.C.) advices have been placed at the disposal of the D.M.S. 3rd Army. Drs Kight & Rendall A.S.C., H.J. relieved from detached duty with the two Pioneer Bat. & replaced by Drs Sumner & Kelly. Inspected the Hospital with St. Gardener the E, b & J Squad and pointed out alterations required — i.e. to make hospital habitable for winter, also the building of a drying room, boil the rise incinerator & quarters for S.A. Surgeons. He promised to speak to his O.C. & arrange about it. House start(?) building near town soon.	
	7.10.17		Weather turned very cold yesterday with pouring rain, so extra blankets issued to Indians among 73 the remainder have not turned up yet. Drs Sullivan and Patrick & S/Lt. H.J. went on # 10 days leave to the United Kingdom yesterday. Capt. Stephen R.A.M.C. (T.C.) reported his departure	

A5834 Wt.W4973/M687 750,000 8/16 D.D.& L. Ltd. Forms/C.2118/13.

WAR DIARY
or
INTELLIGENCE SUMMARY.
(Erase heading not required.)

Army Form C. 2118.

Place	Date	Hour	Summary of Events and Information	Remarks and references to Appendices
Fampoux	7.10.17		to join the 24th Division infantry & was struck off the strength.	
	9.10.17		During the rain yesterday both hospital buildings and the Shoemaker's leaked severely badly and were extremely cold. The R.E. having done nothing although repeatedly applied to for repairs &c. alterations. No stores have been supplied yet. Weather extremely bad wind & rain. Yesterday meeting arranged for starting out the wheelers to runway with the O.C. A.S.C. including Mouton in S. Athens for D.H.Q. Have applied through Capt Hay R.A.M.C. acting D.A.D.M.S for two return stores at once as the material will pay to pieces if kept out in this weather. No 2 g 114 Ford Car refused to start when out on duty with Pte Yule, one cylinder was firing, this was found to be a defective wire.	
	10.10.17		Weather still very wet and stormy. R.Ts of Field Squadron are assisting at getting the roof on the new stables.	
	11.10.17		Went to Ayette to an detachment under S.A.S. Dhan Rag-- on temporary duty with Indian Labor Corps and received a most glowing report from Capt Ween	

Army Form C. 2118.

WAR DIARY
or
INTELLIGENCE SUMMARY.

(Erase heading not required.)

Place	Date	Hour	Summary of Events and Information	Remarks and references to Appendices
Fourques	11.10.17		R.A.M.C. of the good work that the sub assistant surgeon and the detachment from this ambulance had done. The hospital certainly looked very neat and in good order & the S.A.S. and the detachment must have worked extremely hard to get it in that order. They are all asking to return to this unit as soon as they can be relieved. Howe— again asked both the R.2. in charge of works and the A.D.M.S. about the condition of the hospital. The hospital is made of two half Armsen huts and one Ahern. The half Armsen have (tarred) paper for the whole back of the huts, the rops leak in innumerable places and the sides have gaps between the boards where one can pass ones whole hand through. The floor was of mud but the	

Army Form C. 2118.

WAR DIARY
or
INTELLIGENCE SUMMARY.
(Erase heading not required.)

Instructions regarding War Diaries and Intelligence Summaries are contained in F. S. Regs., Part II. and the Staff Manual respectively. Title pages will be prepared in manuscript.

Place	Date	Hour	Summary of Events and Information	Remarks and references to Appendices
Fourpes	12.10.17		unit has worked very hard at getting wood from Grenver dugouts and made wooden floors dado the R.E.s have supplied a certain amount of tarred felt but not sufficient to even recover the roofs let alone the sides, they say they cannot supply the material because no allowance is being made by the division for hospitals they give no assistance as regards carpenters etc. and owing to the Wheeler being away with the O.C. A.S.C. for 2/3 of each month we are left without any skilled labour it is impossible to make a satisfactory or possible hospital in the winter with unskilled labour and insufficient material. I am writing to the A.D.M.S. informing him of the condition of affairs. A new Agent to the R.I.O. 2520 Chuta Singh S. & T. Corps reported his arrival yesterday evening	

WAR DIARY or INTELLIGENCE SUMMARY

Army Form C. 2118.

Place	Date	Hour	Summary of Events and Information	Remarks and references to Appendices
Fouquues	12.10.17		Private Bruce & Act. Corp. Cochrane proceeded on leave to U.K.	
	14.10.17		Sergt. Stevens & Pte. Short reported their arrival from leave yesterday evening with notes showing they had been delayed at Folkestone on the 8th & 9th. Pte Robertson returned this evening. Saw the A.D.M.S. about the hospital and he is making every endeavour to get the division and the R.T. to deal with the matter satisfactorily. Have started to build shelters for officers as their tents are leaking very much exposed & cold, no huts being at present available. 1/Handlar Babu Lall No 7 & A.T.B.C. joined the unit from the Instrs. C.F.A. yesterday	
	17.10.17		Pte Randall & Pte Hussain proceeded on 10 days leave to England. Sergt. Whittingy proceeded on 10 days leave to Wales with Pte Foster	
	20.10.17		The following reported their arrival from leave Pte Roebuck F. Sullivan & Pattrick.	

Army Form C. 2118.

WAR DIARY
or
INTELLIGENCE SUMMARY.
(Erase heading not required.)

Place	Date	Hour	Summary of Events and Information	Remarks and references to Appendices
Frezenberg	22/10/17		Half the Officers shelters have been completed, built of dug out woods and iron sheets from old abandoned German dug outs & trenches. Each quarter being 9ft by 11ft. They are small but dry & warmer than a tent. Dr. Cochrane reported his arrival from leave & Pte House reports on ten days leave to England.	
	24.10.17		Inspected by Col. Morgan A.M.S., D.D.M.S. Cav Corps. He was very pleased with the transport which was then being inspected by the B.I.O. Major Bde. and also with the hospital and congratulated me on them and wishes me to complete the equipment of the Indian Ward with iron bedsteads supplied by the Red Cross. Capt. Haig B.I.O. was also very pleased with the turn out of the transport. Pte Baxter Richardson & Brand returned from leave. Wk. Nyam Martin N2 8 Co. A.B.C. promoted by his Com. commander.	

2353. Wt. W:2541/4454. 700,000. 5/15. D. D. & L. A.D.S.S./Forms/C. 21:8.

Army Form C. 2118.

WAR DIARY
or
INTELLIGENCE SUMMARY.
(Erase heading not required.)

Place	Date	Hour	Summary of Events and Information	Remarks and references to Appendices
Fourques	26/10/17		To 1/September with effect from 1st Aug. 1917	
	28/10/17		S.A.S. Duoan Singh proceeded to Indian native detention hospital for coolie corps at Arleutte to replace S.A.S. Dhan Raj who returned to the unit.	
	31/10/17		Building of officers shelters continued & completed. L/Cpl Smith, B/Cr Kendall returned from leave yesterday. The hospital is always full & during month 38 men returned to duty. R. Hodgson Maj. O.C. Ambala Cav. Fd. Amb.	

Medical —

Original —

War Diary from 1st Nov 1917 to 30th Nov 1917.

Vol: XXXIX

I — Ambala Cav. Fd. Amb.

COMMITTEE FOR THE
MEDICAL HISTORY OF THE WAR
Date — 8 FEB. 1918

AMBALA CAVALRY
FIELD AMBULANCE

R. C. Hodgson Major I.M.S.
Ambala Cav. Fd. Amb.

Army Form C. 2118.

WAR DIARY
or
INTELLIGENCE SUMMARY.
(Erase heading not required.)

Instructions regarding War Diaries and Intelligence Summaries are contained in F.S. Regs., Part II. and the Staff Manual respectively. Title pages will be prepared in manuscript.

Place	Date	Hour	Summary of Events and Information	Remarks and references to Appendices
Fosques	1-3 May /17		The unit is still in bivouacs they have built and have not been supplied by the division with any huts. I have interviewed the O.C. 4th Field Sqn. and reported the matter to the division. The Sanitary Section along side have been supplied with their full compliment of huts by the 4th Field Squadron.	
	4-5 May		Nº 64806 Pte MacEvoy H. R. A.M.C. reported his arrival from 4th Cav. Supply Col. for duty with the ambulance as clerk. Pte Lacey b- (name illegible) Sgn reported his arrival for duty as clerk.	
	5-5 May		Nº 017186 Sgt. McCluskey C. Stores—Sgt (at A.S.C. H.?) reported his arrival for duty vice Stores Sgn Ward (rejoined unit) SCS	
	6-5 May		Sepoy W.O. Fazal Ahmed Khan, 1st Brit. Mahmud Khan were up lined at VII Corps Indian mobile Corps hospital by Bearer (Jangus) & W.O. Bhura Rawnt. # This ambulance supplies all the subordinate medical staff for that except for one orderly supplied by Lucknow C.F.A. Pte. House returned from 10 days leave in U.K.	
	8-5 May		The back of the hospital huts is still made of (tones paper which mas...)	

2353 Wt. W2544/1454 700,000 5/15 D.D.&L. A.D.S.S./Forms/C. 2118.

Army Form C. 2118.

WAR DIARY
or
INTELLIGENCE SUMMARY.

(Erase heading not required.)

Place	Date	Hour	Summary of Events and Information	Remarks and references to Appendices
Fournes	5.3.16		I am extremely cold which I have points out to the R.S. but cannot get Capt. Waller R.S. in charge of busting to do anything at present	
	11.3.16		Pte. Wilson 6th J. Dgn. proceeded on 14 days leave to England	
	14.3.16		I.E. N.S. Yarwood I.M.S. proceeded to report to O.C. 4th Leu Pioneer Bat. for duty with the unit	
	19.3.16		S.A.S. Kissan Singh reported his arrival with the Wheel Orderly Murra Ranu 6, two N.B. Conr, One Washerman & One sweeper from VI Corps reinstated in Indian Hospital Pte. Jones Ivory R.A.M.C. proceeded to report to O.C. walking wounded collecting station Inconyt. C/2 4333 (Macclesfm Sheikh Iphibul Rahman sent sick to Luckmow C.C.S. N= 77306 Kickm at R.E. reported his arrival for duty. The ambulance has been standing to in readiness to move since 9 a.m. this morning Heavy Gun fire heard to the north in direction of Laventie where 3rd Army are making an attack this morning with Tanks.	
	20.3.16			

Army Form C. 2118.

WAR DIARY
or
INTELLIGENCE SUMMARY.
(Erase heading not required.)

Instructions regarding War Diaries and Intelligence Summaries are contained in F.S. Regs., Part II. and the Staff Manual respectively. Title pages will be prepared in manuscript.

Place	Date	Hour	Summary of Events and Information	Remarks and references to Appendices
Fme Concentration area	21/Mr.		Moved to this area, Fme concentration area, at 3.30 A.M. this morning weather cold wet & squally. Dismounted the men three times & halted though the units ahead were dismounted or appeared to have an official halt. No officer at the end of personnel that Pte. Byrne 4 S.C.M.J. would be reported in some what he received an injury to examine the men more than two months previously when on duty. The men were quite resource. About 1800 Yeomen Rations have Physique very poor & most and men exciting Anaemic and Wanting in Endurance fat.	
St Omer	23/Mr.		The unit returned from Steen Fme to St Omer, the division not having been used, to proceed to open Rest Station	
	24/Mr.		2/Lieut. Bahn Lall, A.B.C. was attached early this morning by Brum Bishop at B.C. with a police and necessary 8 Sepoys were very anxious. Behari alleged by L/Naik — and placed under arrest. Summary of Evidence taken and Court Martial applied for.	

2353. Wt. W 2544/1454 700,000 5/15 D.D. & L. A.D.S.S./Forms/C. 2118.

WAR DIARY
or
INTELLIGENCE SUMMARY.

(Erase heading not required.)

Army Form C. 2118.

Place	Date	Hour	Summary of Events and Information	Remarks and references to Appendices
St Omer	29-5-16		Ordered to open rest station for 4th & 5th Div Divisions.	
	30-5-16		Lt General J.M.S. returned the day before yesterday for duty. Horse ambulance orders to proceed with Meerut Pack stretch party has returned with mules party that returned and Division is moving. Rumour there has been a big German attack near Ypres. That the Germans have broken through. Lt Col S. General positions a gun 2nd Cavalry for duty in Hosp. of their own M.O. at present on duty leave in England, left the ambulance to join them 10 P.M. J. Ambulance dealt all patients from Rest Station to armoured off with Division to hope two hours after midnight & have Pack mounted section ready & am moving off with Meerut Pack H.Q. to position for attack at 5 a.m. tomorrow morning.	
Villers Faucon				

E.C. Hodgson Majr J.M.S.

Medical.

(5)

COMMITTEE FOR THE
MEDICAL HISTORY
Date 12 JUL 1918

War Diary from 1.7.6 to 31.7.7.

Vol. XL

1. Ambala Cav. Fd. Amb.

Rukang
for Capt RAMC
O.C. Ambala Cav. Fd. Amb.

AMBALA CAVALRY
FIELD AMBULANCE.
No.........
Date.........

Original
Dec 1917

WAR DIARY or INTELLIGENCE SUMMARY

Army Form C. 2118

Place	Date	Hour	Summary of Events and Information	Remarks and references to Appendices
S'Elien	1st Dec.		Have opened ambulance as Divisional Rest Station for 105 British and 55 Indian patients. Yesterday morning Bearer Behari of 4 B.C, a recent reinforcement attacked Havildar Balu Lal of 4 B.C, a recent reinforcement sent from Lucknow C.T.S. with his Kukri because he said the 1/Havildar had called him vile names and disgraced him before all the Rahas, and wounded him in seven places, one severely practically severing one finger of left hand. If Kukri'd hadn't seized the Behari and with the assistance of others him Balu took away the Kukri Havildar Balu Lal sent to Lucknow C.C.S. only slightly wounded. Behari placed in arrest and after a summary of evidence has been taken a court martial [illeg] very shortly. 10 waggons have been unpacked as the ambulance is no long standing to under motors. Surgeon General Murray this morning inspected the rest hosp.	

WAR DIARY or INTELLIGENCE SUMMARY

Army Form C. 2118.

Place	Date	Hour	Summary of Events and Information	Remarks and references to Appendices
SErun	1st Dec		ambulance altered according to my suggestions to carry & lying or six sitting and approved of it	
Tourpes	4 Dec		Received orders at 12.10 P.M. 30.11.14 to close rest station that patients and from thence marching at earliest possible moment as rapidly as possible to X roads east of Zotrée (?) Loaded all wagons, cleared all patients (20), and closed rest station and was marching by 2.10 P.M. with division to Villers Thourm when we camped for night & received orders to join Mhow Bde. H.Q. with pack mounted section at dawn next morning. Joined Mhow Bde. H.Q. with some difficulty as the same night & arranged where to meet marching with pack mounted section at 3.30 A.M. Ambulance left under command of Capt. Bennie R.A.M.C. Pack mounted section with me under Capt. Long R.A.M.C. marched with Mhow Bde. to Kerpiere where Mhow Bde. attached enemy who had broken through our infantry the previous morning. Indian villages Lys. charged with 11th machine gun squadron from Kerpiere but met with heavy machine gun fire were driven back. The 2nd lancers charging a mile to the East, broke through & drove back the Germans about 2500 yds. The 3rd BC. & I.H. & 3 squadrons were sent in	

WAR DIARY
or
INTELLIGENCE SUMMARY.

(Erase heading not required.)

Army Form C. 2118.

Place	Date	Hour	Summary of Events and Information	Remarks and references to Appendices
Fauquissart	1 Dec		[illegible handwritten entry]	

WAR DIARY
or
INTELLIGENCE SUMMARY

(Erase heading not required.)

Army Form C. 2118.

Place	Date	Hour	Summary of Events and Information	Remarks and references to Appendices
	30.25		How far will townships in which I received enquires (?) and any help on building only issue & equipment for births burials moved from expenses baths & personal shortly. Have seen much with both my Officers & dispose of material also now up to & any batt? of R.B. & A.C. English & S.? have men during in fashion to? Their today turning [Sevilla?]? the disease khejuri to ?? officer & nurse? & another be sickling going from army a month & so light wounds with camp	
	28.		Have been pretty quiet a month a slight troubles have arisen under a young the Bird though regiments temporarily take in & have been lent to ambulance shall be unable to move all vehicles of our advance by more means behind the FA & S.A.L.	
	31.		Recvd Rathew conveying G 5 gyns temp as ? of F 3 & conv. to D. & C. F Indian Force Depths.	

T.C. Hodgson Major RAMC
O.C. Advance C.J.C.S.A

Original:-

Medical / 5

(5)

War Diary from 1st Jany 1918 to 31st Jany 1918.

Vol. XII.

1 Mbl — 1 Cav. Fd. Amce.

COMMITTEE FOR THE
MEDICAL HISTORY OF THE WAR
Date 12 JUL 1919

R.C. Hodgson Lt.Col. I.M.S.
O.C. Ambala Cav. Fd. Amb.

AMBALA CAVALRY
FIELD AMBULANCE.
No.
Date

Army Form C. 2118.

WAR DIARY
or
INTELLIGENCE SUMMARY.
(Erase heading not required.)

Instructions regarding War Diaries and Intelligence Summaries are contained in F. S. Regs., Part II. and the Staff Manual respectively. Title pages will be prepared in manuscript.

Place	Date	Hour	Summary of Events and Information	Remarks and references to Appendices
FOURQUES	1-5 Jan 1915		The Bn. left Chouques (?) and rest station at Doingt for Fourch train sleeves its ambulance & outlines and motor lorries & horses for 18 motor cars.	
	5 Jan		The Bn. transport joined them after arrival on train preparatory to going forward to rejoin first line of Bn. transport. The men have been busy fitting themselves with fresh clothing & new boots & drying & cleaning arms.	
	6 Jan		Brand. Bunda. 24 B.C. has been promoted to Temp. Brig. General. He has 184 promotions with sword, awarded. Lieut. R.H. Jos. rescued(?) will proceed...	
	7 Jan		No 16551.3 Pte Day g. got humiliating fare, reported for duty from Maj C.E. Hodgson went on 14 days leave to England (15th–28th) and Capt R.M. King Rham assumed temporary command of the unit. Bn.	
	8 Jan		Capt the Royd C.T. and his Coy from the Oxys 619, February to J.H.Q. and was replaced by Capt. S.M. Morgan C.T. and from Pte Hatchard Y.Q.	
	9 Jan		Joseph R.H. rescued with difficulty due to new weather.	

WAR DIARY or INTELLIGENCE SUMMARY.

Army Form C. 2118.

(Erase heading not required.)

Place	Date	Hour	Summary of Events and Information	Remarks and references to Appendices
Forgues (b2.c.V.13.a.2.B)	10th		Owing to muddy / intricate [illegible] the [illegible] with received its [illegible] recruits round huts and shelters	
	11th		The Day [illegible]	
	12th		Recent Rugby Match concluded with matches.	
	13th		Presentation of M.S.M. to Sgt S. Glen Reg't and J.S.M. to L/Cpl Brooker by the Canton Corps Commander (Maj Gen Kavanagh) officers and men that all ful personnel C.7 was now to go the [illegible] will	
	14th		rest of Brigade troops in this [illegible] and the slightly greener	
	15th		that they [illegible] to recent	
	16th		Weather has been very bad and prevents [illegible] full house and relaxations sports and [illegible] hold pretty	
	17th		[illegible] of J from Army [illegible] and [illegible] town collected and while there has	
			been sent [illegible] by the [illegible]	

WAR DIARY or INTELLIGENCE SUMMARY

Army Form C. 2118.

Place	Date	Hour	Summary of Events and Information	Remarks and references to Appendices
FOURQUES	Jan 1918 1ˢᵗ		Nothing to record.	
	2ⁿᵈ		The undermentioned officers Capt O'F Brown left the unit to report for duty to O.C. Lucknow C.T.U.	
			The following reinforcements arrived:- A/Cook for Mahomed Sharif, S.T. Exp. Wd 6 duty Abdul Ahmed D/Co. W.L. Servant Thomson Sheoram D/Co/p. Bearer Rikhi, Bishn, Mathuri, W/S Exp. Cook Mahomed Sadiq, S.T. Co/.	
	2 1ˢᵗ		Nothing to record	
	2 2ⁿᵈ		Nothing to record	
	2 3ʳᵈ		Nothing to record	
	2 4ᵗʰ		Lieut Col. T.C. Hodgson, I.M.S. reported his arrival from 14 days leave. Capt Longr R of A.M.C. reported his departure on 14 days leave to U.K. S.A.S. Dhoum May, I.S.M.D. proceeded on 5 days leave to Kanu. One L.D. evacuated sick, being to whom m. V.S.S.	
	2 5ᵗʰ		Surgeon Major F.T. Cooke R.A.M.C. proceeded on 14 days leave to U.K.	
	2 6ᵗʰ		Dʳ Rondel I.A.S.C. proceeded on 14 days leave to U.K.	
	2 8ᵗʰ		Sergt Walkeys F.H., I.A.S.C. evacuated sick with symptoms acute inflam. of meninges	

Army Form C. 2118.

WAR DIARY
or
INTELLIGENCE SUMMARY.

(Erase heading not required.)

Place	Date	Hour	Summary of Events and Information	Remarks and references to Appendices
Fourques	31.1.18		Draw Ray S.A.S. Returned from leave in Paris	
			E.C. Hodgson Lt Col. I.M.S.	
			O.C. Ambulance C.F. of A.	

Medical

Original

War Diary from 1st Feby 1918 to 28th Feby 1918.

Vol. XLII

1 — Ambala Cav. F.A.

COMMITTEE FOR THE
MEDICAL HISTORY OF THE WAR
Date 12 JUL 1918

J. Garrood
Capt. I.M.S.
(Acting)
O.C. Ambala Cav. Fd. Amb.

AMBALA CAVALRY.
FIELD AMBULANCE.

Army Form C. 2118.

WAR DIARY
or
INTELLIGENCE SUMMARY.
(Erase heading not required.)

Instructions regarding War Diaries and Intelligence Summaries are contained in F. S. Regs., Part II. and the Staff Manual respectively. Title pages will be prepared in manuscript.

Place	Date	Hour	Summary of Events and Information	Remarks and references to Appendices
Fauquez	1st Sep		Ambulance hospital closed preparatory to move tomorrow. Hospital (M. Res) Cross & ordnance stores handed over to M.O. from 5th C.F.A. 2nd Cav. Bde who have arrived to take over.	
Harbonnieres	2nd Sept		Unit marched back to Harbonnieres today starting 9.15 A.M. & getting in at 2.30 P.M. distance 17½ miles, no casualties of animals or men.	
Roisquesnil	3rd		Unit started 8.15 A.M. marched 32 miles to Roisquesnil arriving 6 P.M. & billeted here for night, no casualties to animals or men, road bad in parts and very hilly.	
Aumont	4th		Unit marched to final billets here starting 11 A.M. arriving 12.30 P.M. about ten miles. Good billets & quite a good small hospital in small disused Chateau. Opened hospital at once for 6 British beds & 15 Indian.	
	5th		Major Clusky A.S.C. H.T. proceeded on leave 14 days to U.K. on 3rd.	
Aumont	6th		D.r Barrah & Pte Boxall of A.S.C. proceeded on 14 days leave to U.K.	
	8th		Capt. Barry Mackay proceeded on 14 days leave to U.K.	
	10th		Capt. Lang R.A.M.C. & S.M. J.T Cooke R.A.M.C. reported their arrival from 1st Hosp. Stn.	

WAR DIARY
or
INTELLIGENCE SUMMARY
(Erase heading not required.)

Army Form C. 2118.

Place	Date	Hour	Summary of Events and Information	Remarks and references to Appendices
Amara	10/2/18		Capt. Lad ORAMC attached to Field Amb. but kept under command of [illegible]	
	12/2/18		General Hutchs 1st G.O.H. Mesopotamia O.D.O. from at dusk to H.Q.	
	14/2/18		Lt Sordal RSC AS reports his arrival from at dusk flies to H.Q. for Sun	
	6/2/18		Mitchell RAMC wrote his journal from [illegible] for duty with Ambulance	
	17/2/18		Lt. Gill R.C. MT Reports his departure on at dusk leave to H.Q. from	
			Lt Col S.S. Jordan [illegible] proceeds to H.Q. to act as ADMS of 16 Division	
	18/2/18		Lt Col [illegible] RAM took over last Journal Command	
	19/2/18		C attached to hand over	
			Gunnell RN. Evacts Doar and Lieut	OK It Jour replaces Lt Gibbs Williams
			Mitchell, James Cas Jordan	R.C.H.? Run
			Lt Grinnel, has thus noted RGAR of the Division for duty Worker Run	
			Gus Lody, R.C.H. Arrived from base to R.S.H. for	
			Capt (Rush) Wright. R.C.A.T. Proceeds to H.R. on at dusk Leave Run	
	23/2/18		[illegible] Bath Lt N Brown proceeds on 14 days leave to U.K.	
	21/1/18		St Beek M.S.R. USA left to join duties C.H., being replied by C.W. Thompson R.I.A. from that unit	

WAR DIARY or INTELLIGENCE SUMMARY

Army Form C. 2118.

Place	Date	Hour	Summary of Events and Information	Remarks and references to Appendices
	21/2/18		Lt. TITERON. RAMC. reported here for duty from Sialkot. CFA. Three ABC men returned from duty with DHQ.	
	22/2/18		Capt Kemp & entire Indian Personnel left for railhead to go to Tarawda.	
			Capt Thompson took over Company command.	
	23/2/18		Capt. J.R.S. Mackay RAMC reported his arrival from 14 days leave to U.K. Capt J.R's Mackel came with Pre Boatman & Pickandle P Thompson proceeded to rep at Sialkot. CFA for duty. P. Morton Yorke hours by reported his arrival from Cradel. CFA for duty.	
	24/2/18		Parkhester & Lynx Kellum Dragoons proceeded to report to & Freericht for duty. Dr Huggan ASC HT. proceeded to Rwal an HT Company to rep at BATIBAL NSC HT. If Apulchan GS. wagon Capt Farrd reported his arrival from Lucknow CFA for duty. B Sarah P Broall ASC reported arrived from 14 days leave from UK. Drs Park Reanse ASC HT reported arrived from Jethpum CFA for duty.	
	25/2/18		Dr Ranno L proceeded to report to O.C. ASC HT Con Dis for duty	S. Thompson Capt OMMCS

WAR DIARY or INTELLIGENCE SUMMARY

Army Form C. 2118.

Place	Date	Hour	Summary of Events and Information	Remarks and references to Appendices
	25/2/18		Lt Col. E.C. Hodgson reported arrival from D.H.Q. having been temporarily attached to ADMS: On Ship ASC. HT reported his arrival from OT+Q Ordnance. S.T.	
	26/2/18		Nothing to record. S.T.	
	27/2/18		Pte Racey 6th Inniskilling Dragoons proceeded to report to O.C. his unit. S.T.	
	28/2/18		Lt Col E.C. Hodgson I.M.S. proceeded on 14 days leave to U.K. Driver Penrose ASC proceeded to return to Base depôt Havre on being surplus to Establishment. Lt Theron R.A.M.C. proceeded to Lucknow C.F.A. to take over Command of detach there	

JRJohnson Capt RAMC

MEDICAL.

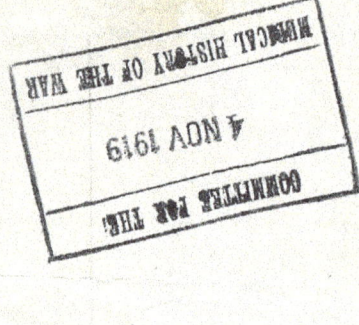

WAR DIARY from 1-3-1918 to 31-3-1918

VOL. XLIII

AMBALA C. F. A.

WAR DIARY
or
INTELLIGENCE SUMMARY.

(Erase heading not required.)

Form C. 2118.

Place	Date	Hour	Summary of Events and Information	Remarks and references to Appendices
France	1/3		During first half of the month the ambulance was	
Egypt	14/3/16		(?) Kantara Reserve with all field personnel, animals on trains to (?) transports, moving there on the 3rd inst. that party remained in camp near (?) till the 9th. They embarked on S.S. Minuteonia (?) on the 13th and disembarking at El Kantara on the 15th. Stones they entrained for TEL EL KEBIR Camp. The British personnel, animals and transport came via Still left Marseille and Alexandria arriving here in the 11th & (?) on the 18th March. No other items of the unit was to Egypt but the Hospital Wing is operating in a few weeks time. (?)	

WAR DIARY
or
INTELLIGENCE SUMMARY.

(Erase heading not required.)

Place	Date	Hour	Summary of Events and Information	Remarks and references to Appendices
TELEL- KEBIR	14/3/15		Capt R McKay Rennie joined at TELEL-KEBIR E.E.F. W/A all personnel of 1st unit and all were allotted to sheds — met Lieut Veffy, my superior in S.M.O. Tel-el-Kebir EEF Lt Col H. Heath (Cav). There have been several cases of enteric fever amongst troops lately through Guinea Pig now have to use sterilised 1 p.m.	
	17/3/15		All Hubbled tents + 1 circ. with horses, but hospital at the 25ε H.T. tent, 2 lg cas. you listen to a & been turned cal + descends with them out of the wagon + wounded — the horse though WC are passing a avenue, smart, at 4.10 a.m. a mule strap and the railway bog Les to smoothed — lan down Singapore lads, arsenal, N.S.W. tents — need to you are e.s.D. tents S.M.B. Sulh of G te.	
	19/3/15		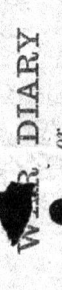	

WAR DIARY
or
INTELLIGENCE SUMMARY.
(*Erase heading not required.*)

Instructions regarding War Diaries and Intelligence Summaries are contained in F. S. Regs., Part II. and the Staff Manual respectively. Title pages will be prepared in manuscript.

[illegible]y Form C. 2118.

Place	Date	Hour	Summary of Events and Information	Remarks and references to Appendices
TEL-EL-KEBIR	19/3/18		patients. In addition to commanding this unit I attend to sick and sanitation of Kantara Bas Details - about 350 men and [illegible] others including this unit. Attention to Sanitation takes a lot of time. Bucket latrines are used, the excreta being burnt with stone oil, tibben or [illegible]. Rm	
	20/3/18		Baths cannot be supplied as water is scarce but personnel may bathe in bath houses taking water in buckets. Rm	
	21/3/18		S.M.O. visited the camp with O.C. Eg. Sanitary Section. Demand was made on O.S.C. for tins for fire buckets or for permission to return empty tins for this purpose but was refused. Rm	
	22/3/18		Nothing to record Rm	
	23/3/18		Nothing to record Rm	
	24/3/18		Fire buckets mentioned above 21-3-18 obtained. Rm	
	25/3/18		G.O.C. Egyptian Forces inspected camp and hospital Rm	
	26/3/18		British and Indian personnel paid. Wd. Sgt. Abdul Rahman evacuated sick to	

WAR DIARY or INTELLIGENCE SUMMARY

Army Form C. 2118.

(Erase heading not required.)

Instructions regarding War Diaries and Intelligence Summaries are contained in F.S. Regs., Part II. and the Staff Manual respectively. Title pages will be prepared in manuscript.

Place	Date	Hour	Summary of Events and Information	Remarks and references to Appendices
EL EL KEBIR	2/3/16		To Sublet O.Th. with recommendation for transfer home. Rae	
"	27/3/16		Two men arrived as reinforcement to Sublet C/O on from Rae to Cavalry S.a.Staim Sgt attached for temporary duty att. 166. I F.A. W.O. I/c Sgt attached for temporary duty with 157 February Hospital Rae.	
"	28/3/16		Order received from Div. HQ to detail 10% of Indian personnel for leave to India. Few weeks from arrival at depot, being granted. Eight men not submitted to personnel of 77. Rec.	
"	29/3/16		Nothing to record. Rae	
"	30/3/16		Nothing to record. Rae	
"	31/3/16		Ward Asst Abdul Rahman admitted will returned to depot on unfit for further Active Service Burn Blair returned from Hospital Rae	

Anthony Cpt. R.A.V.C.
O.C. Autopsit C.T.C.
2/4/16

www.ingramcontent.com/pod-product-compliance
Lightning Source LLC
Chambersburg PA
CBHW081237170426
43191CB00034B/1847